OWNING A GREAT BUSINESS

Book Design by Design Dynamics

Published by Lorin Young
Copyright © 2016 by Lorin Young
Irvine, California, 92614

All rights reserved. No part of this publication may be reproduced, distributed, or transmitted in any form or by any means, including photocopying, recording, or other electronic or mechanical methods, without the prior written permission of the publisher, except in the case of brief quotations embodied in critical reviews and certain other noncommercial uses permitted by copyright law.

Printed in the United States of America

copyright © 2016 by Lorin Young
ISBN-9798371497208

All rights reserved, including the right to reproduce this book and/or portions thereof in any form.

CONTENTS
OWNING A GREAT BUSINESS
7 ORGANIZING PRINCIPLES SO YOURS IS ONE OF THEM

CHAPTER	PAGE
Preface	1
Introduction – Producing a Winning Business Formula	5
1. The Difficulties of Owning a GREAT Business	11
2. 7 Organizing Principles for Owning a Great Business	17
3. 1st Organizing Principle: WHO? *(Target Customer)*	31
4. 2nd Organizing Principle: WHAT? *(Product)*	37
5. 3rd Organizing Principle: WHEN? *(Place^1)*	47
6. 4th Organizing Principle: WHERE? *(Place^2)*	57
7. 5th Organizing Principle: WHY? *(People)*	69
8. 6th Organizing Principle: HOW? *(Promotion + Packaging)*	81
9. 7th Organizing Principle: PROFITS! *(Price)*	91
10. A Few More Nuggets of Wisdom	101
Conclusion – Owning a GREAT Business is Within Your Reach	119
Appendix: Confirming What I Need to do Differently Exercise	123
About the Author	131
Source Citations	134
Index	136

WISHING YOU BLUE SKIES AND CLEAR ROADS AHEAD.

LORIN YOUNG

PREFACE

PRODUCING A WINNING BUSINESS FORMULA

Over my life I have done a lot of different things and had a wide array of experiences. Yet nothing I have ever done is more challenging than being a small business owner, operating a million-dollar business without a financial safety net. Nothing pushes me harder to work as smart as I can, knowing that my life's savings and the financial security of my family and employees is at risk every day through the decisions I make regarding my business.

Can you relate to these feelings? Are you working as hard as you can for as long as you can each day? Perhaps you are feeling frustrated, angry and exhausted? Trust me, I know just how you feel.

In February of 2009, I lost my job as Vice President of Marketing and Sales at Veterinary Pet Insurance. At first, I thought my unemployment wouldn't last long. I'm a hard worker, with a solid pedigree and track record of producing results; yet, I remained jobless. In July of 2009 I decided that instead of trying to persuade others to give me a job during the great recession, I would create my own.

SUCCESS IS A PROCESS

My decision grew from the realization of how much I love the process of building businesses. So why not build my own? This thought led me to redeploy our retirement savings into establishing my own business. I was confident that I knew what it took to build a business.

I have an MBA and a BA in marketing management and have worked for nearly twenty years in a variety of roles for two very different Fortune 100 companies. I believe in myself. I know I have the experience, wisdom and commitment to successfully build my own business.

With the full support of my wife, we took our life savings and put it at higher risk. Our thinking was that we could continue to entrust our savings to the financial wizards on Wall Street, who were clearly struggling in 2009 and again in 2016, or we could fully entrust ourselves with the responsibility to grow our net worth.

We chose ourselves—and today, our business is worth six times what it was when we started out.

BELIEVE IN YOURSELF

Running a small business is the hardest yet most satisfying work of my career. As the owner of Design Dynamics, I continue to learn the principles of what works, and what gets in the way. *The target audience for this book is business leaders, just like you, who are working hard with passion and purpose, yet are unsatisfied with the results.* You want to own a great business, yet recognize that your business isn't in that category yet. My goal for this book is to help you and those you employ enjoy greater success in all aspects of business.

FEAR OF MISTAKES

During my corporate years, I worked in the functions of sales, marketing, human resources, finance and operations. As I look back on my corporate years, one thing that stands out to me is the countless hours I spent in meetings, interacting with all levels of bureaucracy, discussing what we should do.

Small meetings and large meetings—why so many meetings? Because bureaucrats are afraid of making a mistake, and as a result, are afraid of making a decision in the moment.

The bureaucrat's fear of making a mistake is one of the key differences that exist between large and small businesses. In a large company, a mistake can derail your career or cause you to lose your sponsorship. But the resources of a large company can usually absorb the financial hit of a single, bad decision; whereas, in a smaller company, a poor strategic decision can mean the loss of your business.

In either case, the fear of making a mistake can lead to decision paralysis.

CONFIDENT DECISIONS

The successes I enjoyed at PPG Industries, Inc. and Nationwide Insurance were grounded in approaching each function I worked in from a "decision science" perspective. I learned that the best way to make great things happen is through framing the issues in such a way that a confident decision can be made.

Nothing great ever happens when people are unsure, indecisive or afraid. Great businesses are continuously being built utilizing organizing principles that result in great decisions.

SMART STRATEGIES

As a small business owner, I traded the battle with internal bureaucracies to get things done for a struggle against limited resources. In both cases, I have come to appreciate why people get less-than-desired results from their hard work. The breadth of experiences I have enjoyed over my career has helped me to identify strategies for avoiding costly and time-consuming mistakes. I believe the answer to achieving better business results lies in the insightful application of key guiding principles that help produce a winning business formula.

Thank you for allowing me to share some of the wisdom I have gleaned in life. You will find this book and framework to owning a great business really works, if you work it.

Often we buy books or courses, fully intending to put the concepts into practice. Please commit to reading, adapting, and practicing the principles. You have worked hard and deserve to have your energy result in you owning a great business.

Respectfully,

Lorin Young

Founder, Keystone Revenue Solutions, Inc.
Owner, Design Dynamics

"The spirit of exploration, whether it be of the surface of the earth, the vastness of space, or the principles of living greatly, includes developing the capacity to face trouble with courage; disappointment with cheerfulness; and triumph with humility.

God left the world unfinished for man to work his skill upon.

He left the electricity in the cloud, the oil in the earth.

He left the rivers unbridged and the forests unfelled and the cities unbuilt.

God gives to man the challenge of raw materials, not the ease of finished things.

He leaves the pictures unpainted and the music unsung and the problems unsolved, that man might know the joys and glories of creation."

THOMAS S. MONSON

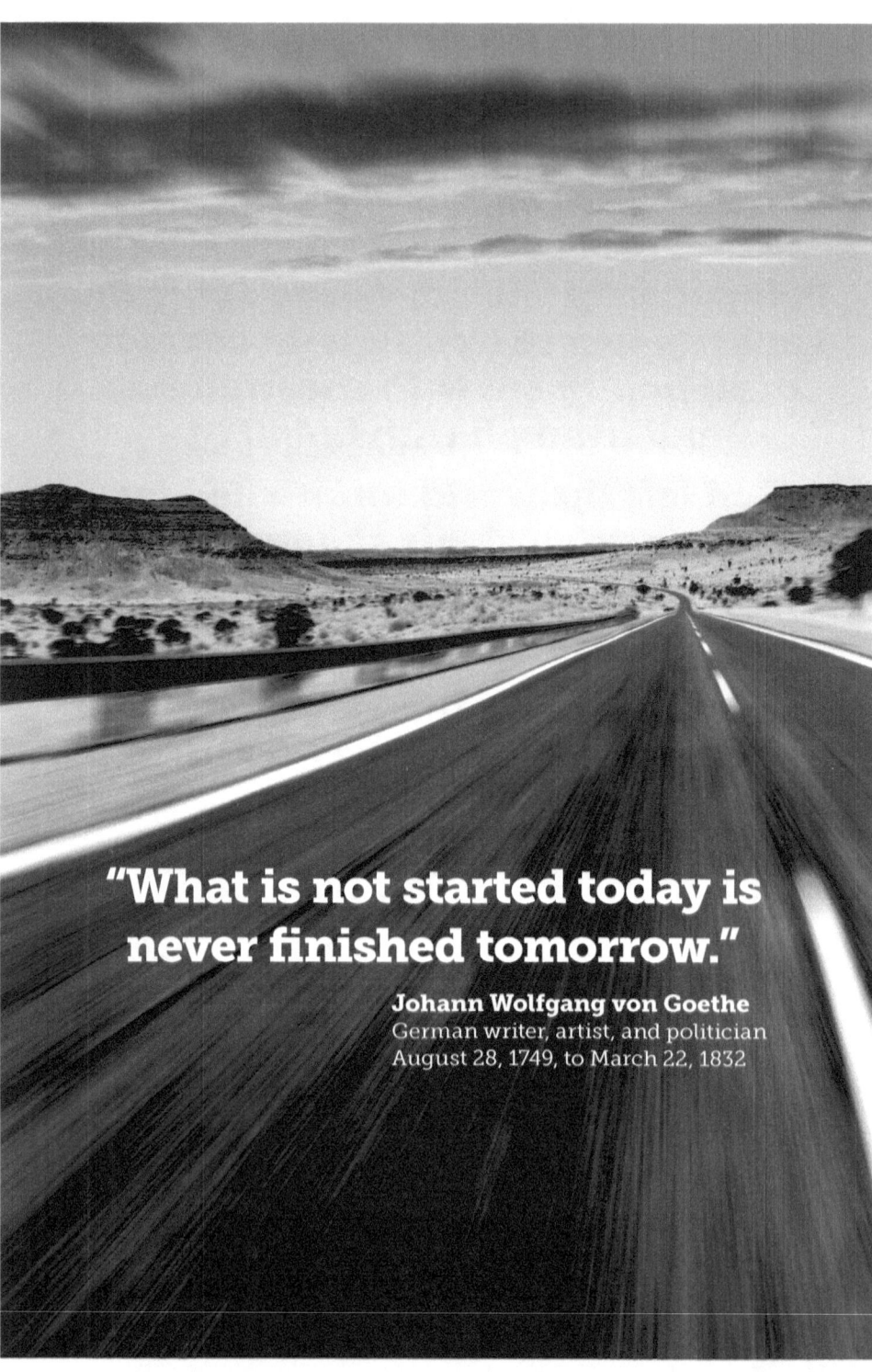

INTRODUCTION

PRODUCING A WINNING BUSINESS FORMULA

YOU ARE READING THIS BOOK FOR ONE OF A HANDFUL OF REASONS:

- You are a small business owner working hard on your business, yet are unsatisfied with your results.
- You want to start your own business and want to know the key principles to follow for success.
- You have a good business, yet you know you need to do things differently to survive, and you aren't sure how best to proceed.
- You are climbing the corporate ladder of a large company and believe that if you acted more like a small business owner, you could contribute even more to your company.
- You are a student of business and you want to understand how it works from a small business owner's perspective—one who started out in corporate America.

No matter your reason for reading this book, I am honored that you are investing your time in learning how to unlock the seven organizing principles for owning a great business. I realize as I grow older that I stop reading more books than I finish, because the writer fails to hold my attention. This failure to grasp and keep my attention is often caused by the author's repeating the same thought, in similar ways, throughout each chapter.

In this book you will find that each chapter is crafted along a unique line of thinking. The benefit of this book is in learning to use the 7-P Framework to reflect on the strengths, weaknesses, opportunities, and threats that exist across your business.

CONCENTRATED TRUTH

The key to business success lies in organizing the truth we gather into simple statements of principle—statements that we can act on. I define principles as "concentrated truth, packaged for application to a wide variety of circumstances." You know you have unlocked a true principle when you find clarity in the decisions you must make, even under the most confusing circumstances.

In fact, this sense of clarity derives directly from the process of organizing the information we know, and applying it to the decision we are entrusted to make. For example, let's consider the strategies of seasoned detectives who commonly use the information-gathering formula of "who, what, when, where, why, and how," in solving crimes. The same is true for newspaper reporters and mystery writers, who use the 5W's + H to organize facts, thoughts, and ideas before they begin to write.

In my career, I've learned that every business is unique, yet know that every smart business leader relies on some fundamental information-organizing formula when making important business decisions.

STAYING POWER

One of my favorite ways to unwind at the end of a long day is to watch procedural crime shows like -----, Law & Order, and Elementary, with my wife of over thirty years. Identified below are the top ten crime shows from the 1990's. To make this list, each series had to have aired at least half its run in the 90's, or to have run a minimum of five seasons in the 90's.

As you look at this list of shows, I would encourage you to consider the staying power each show had. The writers for these shows were great at telling stories that kept us tuning in   to their shows for years. The producers were skilled at marshalling the resources needed to tell the entertaining stories their writers created and their actors portrayed.

From the network's point of view, any television episode only exists to entice people to watch the commercials. This is why the odds are stacked against the creators of a show. If their show gets picked up, the cost to produce these forty-minute television episodes is about three million. The show will shoot over eight days, averaging roughly five minutes of airtime per day of production. The typical script for a one-hour show is fifty-five pages in length.

OVERCOME ODDS

Let us appreciate the odds these show creators had to overcome to get on the air. A major TV network executive will review close to three thousand pitches over the course of the June-through-October pitching season. Through the pitching process, they will buy roughly a hundred drama series. Of those they buy, they will commission about twenty-five to go to script. Out of the twenty-five that go to script, they might shoot five pilots. And of the five pilots produced, they are likely to buy only three or fewer shows, which will be funded for production and will air for at least a few episodes.

TOP 10 CRIME DRAMAS FROM THE 1990'S

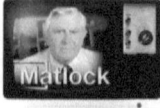

Before any of the top 10 crime shows listed on the previous page made it to TV stardom, they survived this pitch-to-pilot process. Throughout all of the hard work done by the shows' creators as they moved from script, to pilot, to their first year on the air, there was never any guarantee of success, or any idea of how long their shows would "live."

RELATABLE STORY

To best appreciate how skilled these writers are at pulling a story together, consider the golden age of TiVo and other TV recording devices. Do you ever find yourself fast-forwarding through the commercials, only to back-up because you skipped too far ahead? You back-up, and even watch part of a TV commercial, just so you don't miss a key part of the story that may give you an important clue to solving the crime before the hero does. That's how captivating these shows really are. Why? They tell us a relatable, engaging story.

While each of these top ten crime shows had different premises, characters, and settings, the writers all applied the same formula of *"who, what, when, where, why, and how"* to each week's show script. They use this fundamental information management formula in their storytelling to keep us coming back to watch their show through the commercial breaks, and from season-to-season.

CONNECT WITH YOUR AUDIENCE

These shows were successful because we connected with how the crime solvers identified the *"who, what, when, where, why and how"* in solving a crime. Another point to appreciate is that we each probably tuned in to enjoy very different shows. My wife and I faithfully watched five of the top ten crime shows of the 1990's each week, but we never watched two others, while discovering one of these hit crime dramas later in reruns.

The same is true for our respective businesses. Not everyone who could potentially buy from us will. It's easy to compare people buying from your business, to TV viewers tuning in each week to watch their favorite show. It's just that, instead of purchasing products for money, they are committing their time to the network carrying their favorite show. The "win" for the consumer is mindless entertainment. The "win" for the network is a loyal audience willing to watch commercials, for which the network is collecting millions in advertising dollars.

RELATIONSHIPS START WITH CONNECTIONS

What can we draw from this comparison? People will buy from you because they connect with the storyline you have created for your business. When they knowingly pass on your offer or ignore your business altogether, you have failed to make a connection. And, a failed connection means no business. Just like a TV show will be canceled if it loses too many viewers, your business will cease to exist if people don't buy your product or choose your service. One of my goals is to show you how to keep this from happening.

Before you begin to read *Owning a GREAT Business: 7 Organizing PRINCIPLES so Yours is One of Them!* consider the working title I had for this book: *"Seven Fatal Flaws in Business and How You Can Avoid Them."* I originally focused my thinking on these seven fatal flaws to help flush out the slow killers to established businesses, and immediate killers for start-ups.

The key for me in this initial working title was the phrase, *"How You Can Avoid Them."* My intent in writing this book has always been to help hardworking business leaders enjoy greater success. I love the game of business and know that like any game, it's a lot more fun to play when you know how to win! Winning ultimately comes down to knowing what problems and mistakes to avoid, as well as what strategies to follow.

AVOID FATAL FLAWS

What I knew as the "foundational problems" associated with each of the seven fatal flaws identified in my early drafts of this book began to show up to me through the revision and refining process as "organizing principles." What I better-appreciate now is that when organizing principles are skipped in the business decisions you make every day, they later manifest as flaws over time.

I found this particularly to be true when the hard decisions you make don't produce the desired results. You start blindly trying new and different things, because you know your business is in trouble. If you're like me, you don't have much of a financial safety net. Your margins are constrained by the market, and that makes the balancing of payables and receivables an Olympic-size task.

OWN A GREAT BUSINESS

One of my goals in life is to own a great business. What I have learned in trying to make my business great is that a single, small decision poorly made, isn't fatal.

A single, small decision poorly made, isn't fatal.

Over the years, I have not been 100% perfect in my decision making for our business. I've made some decisions I wish I had made sooner, others I wish I had never made, and many that I'm very glad I made and passionately pursued.

In refining this book for publication, what I came to appreciate is that thus far, I have been very blessed. I have been able to avoid the cumulative effect of poor decision making. I attribute this to being cognizant of the organizing business principles derived from knowing the "who, what, when, where, why, and how" of my business. As a result, I've been able to protect my cash flow as I invest the money required to grow my business in product, promotion and place. I've proven to myself that these organizing principles really work, and now I'm sharing them with you.

PLAN FOR ONGOING SUCCESS

While the top ten crime shows from the 1990s aired on different days and on different networks, they had one thing in common: eventually, they all came to an end. But this doesn't have to happen to your business. Read this book and commit to following the principles for at least one year. So you don't become that business owner who has to shut down operations because you ignored one of the seven organizing principles for owning a great business.

Another factor to consider is what happens when the creativity and credibility begin to fade out of a TV show. The phrase "jumped the shark" was invented after the Happy Days episode in which Fonzie jumps over a shark on water skis. While it was certainly memorable, some entertainment critics feel that the show never recovered its credibility after that episode. Similarly,

Repeated violation of any of the seven fatal flaws will cause your business to lose credibility...

repeated violation of any of the seven organizing principles for doing great business will cause your business to lose credibility, which is the beginning of the end for your business, and possibly, your career.

RETAIN CREDIBILITY

The key to our respective businesses' success is doing something every single day to stay relevant to our customers. We do this by continuing to deliver what they need and want, before they stop buying from us or turning to us for solutions.

I encourage you to consider the importance of taking intentional action as you continue to change the way you think and plan your business. Your goal should be to do something different that is foundational to achieving greater success.

You want to succeed or you would not have started a business. You want to be the catalyst for success not the reason your business fails. You don't want your business to "jump the shark" because you violated one of the key principles that underpins owning a great business.

Don't let this happen. Make the good business decision to read on and incorporate the principles in your daily considerations. Share with your employees and make it a team effort to bring greatness to your business dealings.

"Experience is a hard teacher because she gives the test first, the lesson afterward."

Vernon Law
Pittsburgh Pirates Baseball Pitcher
March 12, 1930

CHAPTER ONE

DIFFICULTIES OF OWNING A GREAT BUSINESS

According to research by the U.S. Small Business Administration, a new business has a 50% chance of making it to its five-year milestone and only a 33% chance of making it to the ten-year mark. The hard reality is that for every ten businesses that start, five will fail in the first five years, and two more will not make it to their ten-year anniversaries. Altogether, this means that only three of the original ten will remain viable beyond their first decade.

ACCOUNTING YOUR CASH

Most people believe and will tell you that running out of cash is the primary reason businesses fail. Have you ever had too much month at the end of your money? In 1986, this was the number one takeaway for me from Professor Woodall's Accounting 101 class, "When you're out of cash, you're out of business." Cash flow from operations is the number one sustainability metric for any business: Literally, Accounting 101.

Running out of cash is a surefire way to put a "Closed" sign on the door. Yet, I would argue that the number one reason businesses fail is because people stop buying.

PEOPLE STOP BUYING

The U.S. government study on "Why Customers Stop Buying" identified the following reasons why people ***Stop Buying***:

- **4% are gone.** They move, are promoted, transfer, divorce, or die. They are simply no longer in a position to make any more buying decisions in that geographic area.
- **5% change suppliers, based on the recommendation of a friend or business associate**. Someone else has persuaded them to give their business to one of your competitors. (Ouch!)
- **9% change because of a true competitive advantage available through your competitor, one that your business does not offer**. More often than not, the "benefit" is a lower price point.
- **14% change because they are unhappy with your service or product**. This typically happens when you sell them something that's not the right fit for them. You are better off not making that particular sale, than selling something that's totally wrong for the customer. They will trust you more when they understand that you are watching out for, and choosing, their needs over your own. (And maybe they'll remember that, and seek out your business in the future.)
- **68% stop buying from you because the customers feel that your employees don't care about them or their company.** People will stop buying from you based on how they are treated. Simply put, your employees need to show that they care about the customer and their experience with your company.

The numbers are clear: sixty-eight out of one hundred customers who stop buying, can be retained if they know you care whether they return to buy from your business again. People want and need to feel valued and appreciated for the money they spend with you.

50% OF BUSINESSES SUCCEED

If you accept that fifty out of one hundred new businesses fail, then mathematically you know that 50% of new businesses succeed. The ultimate question is which side of this 50/50 equation will your business be on?

You can better ensure your success when you understand that your chances dramatically improve when you capitalize on the seven organizing principles for doing great business!

It is true some businesses ultimately fail for many different reasons, but yours does not need to fall in this category. I believe business leaders fail their businesses when they don't understand their customer fundamentals with clarity and precision.

It's as if they are leading their business through a black-box maze, making all decisions, both minor and vitally important, in the dark. This walking with a blindfold around your eyes can result in one or more of the "red alerts" listed below of this first figure:

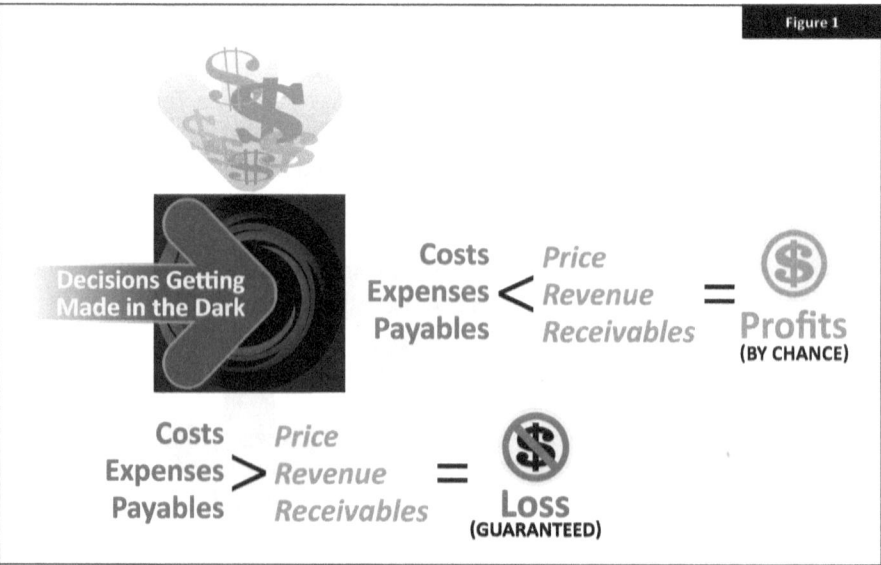

Figure 1

Whether working for a large or small company, the core definition of business is the same: *It is the exchange of value that comes through serving a need or satisfying a want, at a profit.*

This exchange of value only occurs when the following fundamentals are met:
- **Your price points are greater than your costs**
- **Your revenues are greater than your expenses**
- **Your receivables are greater than your payables**

Whether you are a small or large business, your operations will shut down if these business fundamentals are not met.

DECISION MAKING

One of the big differences between a large and small company is in the division of labor, and in who is making the decisions required in running a business. In a big company, the work is spread across a number of different specialists with narrow job definitions, reporting up through multiple levels of management, and dependent on direction.

At Design Dynamics, a smaller business, I'm personally touching every single decision you'll see identified below.

Notice that within this box of decisions there is none associated with family, health, or hobbies. This is because small business ownership requires so much of us. One of the fundamental truths about being a business owner is that you can't pay someone to love your business like you do. You need to have your finger on the pulse of everything and everyone who is involved in your business.

We aren't like CEOs for large companies, with layers of hierarchy separating us from the employees in the trenches, who are serving our customers.

As you look at this second figure, consider how insulated your Fortune 100 CEO is from the vast majority of decisions needing to be dealt with. In a small business, there is no decision buffer. The good news is that I can make decisions that allow me to move quickly and efficiently, because I don't need to wait for my boss to tell me what I'm "allowed" to do. This is good news for you too.

Figure 2

YOU ARE YOUR BUSINESS

The bad news is that I'm not insulated from angry customers or frustrated employees. If you call *949.870.3320* and ask for Lorin Young, you will get me.

If you called my insurance carrier of the last twenty-five years, Nationwide, (also an old employer of mine), at 1.877.OnYourSide (*1.877.669.6877*) and ask for the CEO, you would never be connected with him directly. He is too insulated in his office to be bothered with customer or employee calls. He has thousands of people in his organization to handle that for him.

> *...highly compensated people are pulled in multiple directions, and frequently wrestle with complex decision...*

Don't get me wrong. I'm not assuming it's easy being the CEO of a Fortune 100 company. These highly compensated people are pulled in multiple directions, and frequently wrestle with complex decisions.

What I am saying is, they don't face the variety of issues and in-the-moment pressures of resolving problems in the way that a small business owner like you does. Large company executives will call another meeting so they have time to review the work of others. They aren't burdened with having to step in and serve an immediate customer need, or resolve an employee issue, while thinking about how to grow their sales or pay their bills on time.

DECIDE HOW TO DECIDE

Another challenge that keeps small business owners from achieving greater success is the absence of a clear decision making process. Bureaucracies are famous for their rigid approach to making large to small decisions. Small business owners are forced to make the majority of their decisions on the fly as they bounce from issue to issue. The lack of a clear decision making process will result in missed opportunities or the ultimate consequence of poor decision making, running out of cash.

> *The lack of a clear decision making process will result in missed opportunities...*

What happens to your business when you run out of cash? You go out of business. What happens to your business when people don't buy from you? The same thing: you go out of business.

PROTECT AND PROFIT

You can protect yourself from these issues by using the 7-P Framework to help you think through the decision consideration you are wrestling with.

While cash is king, this book is not about improving your ability to manage cash, nor about how cash-flow management is a critical success factor for your business. The mistakes I see business leaders make occur along the way, long before the brutal day of financial collapse.

If you accept that the number one reason businesses fail is because people stop buying from them, then I encourage you to read on, to be introduced to the seven organizing principles (7-P) for owning a great business.

The 7-P Framework will anchor your decisions on true principles, so you can avoid the problems associated with people not buying from your business. If you want to appreciate a broader review of why businesses fail, see the Appendix, beginning on page 123, for an in-depth summary and exercise.

> *"Some people are so busy learning the tricks of the trade that they never learn the trade."*
>
> **VERNON LAW**

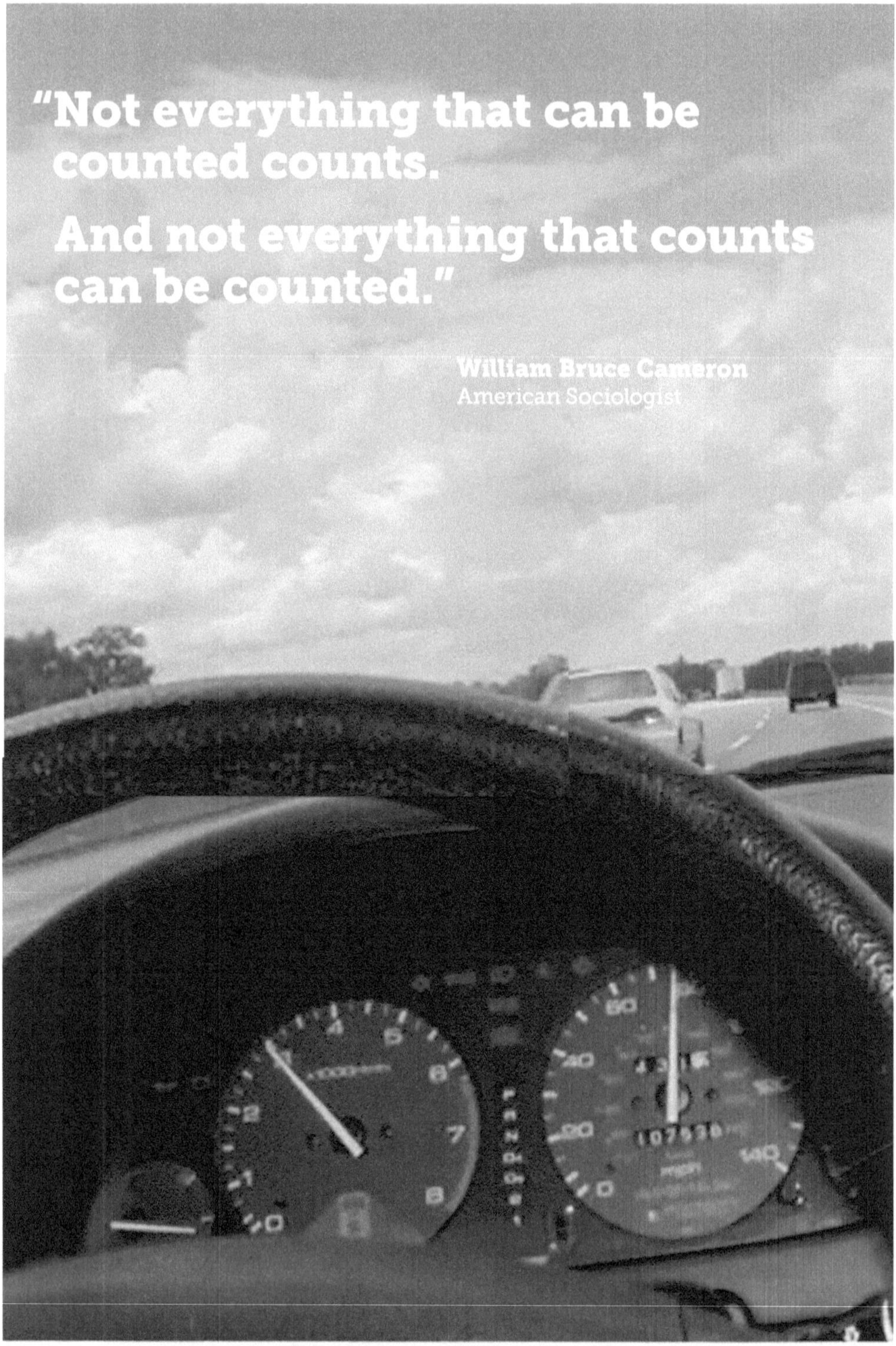
"Not everything that can be counted counts.
And not everything that counts can be counted."
William Bruce Cameron
American Sociologist

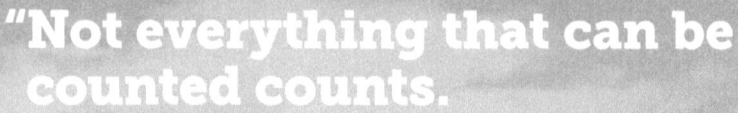

CHAPTER TWO

7 ORGANIZING PRINCIPLES FOR OWNING A GREAT BUSINESS FRAMEWORK

Running a great business is similar to producing an entertaining crime show that has been on the air for years. This analogy has been helpful to guide me in making long-term decisions, and hopefully, you too will benefit.

Both involve putting forth considerable time and effort in defining the "who, what, when, where, why and how" behind the story you want to tell. When we get these answers just right, our businesses run better and smarter. The end result is a steady flow of

> **When we get these answers just right, our businesses run better and smarter.**

satisfied customers who keep coming back, and who will refer us to others. Think about how many times you have enjoyed a show and then recommended it to others.

NO SHORTCUTS TO SUCCESS

When we shortcut the work required to make smart decisions for our business, it is often because we skipped this fundamental information organizing formula. As business owners, we often get so tangled up in the day-to-day that we miss important opportunities.

Remember the time as a teenager you put off doing your homework assignment and then you ended up cramming the night before to get it done? You probably hoped you'd get lucky, and you would not get caught by your teacher. But in reality, those chances were slim. Most teachers can easily spot those tricks, and your grade for the assignment probably reflected how well you completed your work. And you learned that shortcutting your homework assignments rarely results in "A" grades.

PRODUCT, PRICE, PROMOTION AND PLACE

As a small business owner, doing your homework means learning to follow the best frameworks for success. Starting my career in marketing and sales, I learned early on to filter many of my business recommendations through the 4 Ps in marketing: product, price, promotion and place.

However, what I have found over the years is that the 4 Ps are insufficient for creating real clarity in identifying the specific things I needed to do to grow my business. It's true that the 4 Ps are foundational for selling any product, yet I found myself desiring a better mental model to think strategically about my business.

7-P FRAMEWORK MORE ACTIONABLE

My desire to grow my own business at a faster pace led me to identifying the 7-P Framework, and using its principles to realize my goal. In applying this framework, I saw an immediate change in how I approached the decisions I made every day. You will begin to recognize and quick correct how a failure to think through the implications of your business decisions may be holding you back from achieving better results.

FATAL FLAWS TO AVOID

This is what led me to identify the original seven "fatal flaws" I see so many business leaders make. There are a host of reasons that can cause a business to ultimately fail. It has been my experience that the early stages of failure are rooted in this fundamental concept: a failure to understand the firm's customer basics with clarity and precision.

Businesses that fail have not done their information gathering and organizing homework.

This is especially true as they relate to the customer's decisions to choose their business over their competitors. Businesses that fail have not done their information gathering and organizing homework.

Once you know who your customer is, what problem they are trying to solve, when they are most likely to need your help, and where they will want to transact business, you can define the why and how they should value what you are offering, at a profitable price point. While this concept may seem simple on the surface, it amazes me how many business leaders fail to grasp these business fundamentals clearly. As a result they fail to apply them to the small to large decisions they make every day.

Violating these seven organizing principles can hold business leaders back from achieving greater success:

1. Not knowing precisely **WHO** should or will buy what they have to offer.
2. Not knowing **WHAT** problem their customers are trying to solve, by purchasing from them.
3. Not knowing **WHEN** their target will want or need to have the product or service offered.
4. Not knowing **WHERE** their customer will want to make the purchase.
5. Not knowing the **WHY** behind the customer's purchasing decision, and not communicating this information to their employees.
6. Not knowing **HOW** the buyer will benefit from the product or service they purchase.
7. None of your answers to the 5 W's + H matters if they don't result in a **PROFIT**.

CHANGE IS NECESSARY FOR SUCCESS

These fundamental business questions often remain unanswered or the answers become less clear over time. In *Psychology Today*, the quote associated with the definition of insanity—"doing something over and over again and expecting a different result"—has been variously attributed to Albert Einstein, Ben Franklin and Mark Twain.

No matter who said it, the premise is significant. If you want a different result, you have to implement changes. And most humans find change to be... difficult.

> *...innovations change how people react to their environments, and these interruptions to our habits are becoming more disruptive...*

We live in a rapidly changing world that often requires us to make these adaptions, to do things differently than we did previously. New methods of doing business are being invented daily.

Technological innovations change how people react to their environments, and these interruptions to our habits are becoming more disruptive. Consider how frequently you upgrade your smartphone to take advantage of the latest new features, or simply to have the latest and greatest phone?

Experts believe we're undergoing the most rapid period of change in human civilization. Change is inevitable, and as our business and technology markets evolve, with or without us, our ability to continue to do as we have always done and achieve the same results disappears. The reality of failing to evolve as our environments evolve results in working harder to hold on to what we have, as it slowly slips away from us.

STEP BACK FOR LONG RANGE VIEW

What I'm offering in the *Seven Organizing Principles for Owning a Great Business* is a core principles framework to help you take a step back from the day-to-day hamster-wheel of your business.

Why do I advise a step back? Because you need to pause occasionally throughout the year to reflect on what's working well, where are you getting stuck, and what should you be doing differently to improve your business.

This is the only way you will begin to see your business differently. Until you learn to see your business through new eyes, you will continue to do what you have always done, while your customers' needs and wants change without you.

The 7-P Framework is an easy-to-use tool that helps you look at your business in a new way, especially when you feel you are falling behind. It is principle-driven; to help you organize your thoughts and use them to create insights you can act on immediately.

ADOPT ABILITY TO ADAPT

This is key. Successful evolution can be defined as the ability to adapt, well, and quickly. More often than not, the people buying from you aren't looking for extra work, nor do they want to foolishly part with their hard earned money.

Let's review another key to business success: your customer has a problem to be solved, or a need to be met. The question is, "will you, or one of your competitors, satisfy your customer?"

This is the fundamental reason that you are marketing, selling, producing and distributing your goods and services. The problem is on whom, when and where do you focus your limited resources. You have a great product to sell; yet you don't want to waste money promoting your business, while failing to make a sale. Because that, my friends, will cause you to go out of business.

The remaining chapters in this book will help you to make better decisions that will result in your business selling more products and services to people who need and want them. As you read each chapter, you will develop insights via the 7-P framework that will create clarity on what you need to do, and what you should no longer do.

WHAT TO DO/WHAT NOT TO DO

Good business strategy is just as much about knowing what not to do, as much as deciding what to do. But great strategy is only realized when you execute it successfully.

As you study the seven organizing principles for owning a great business, I encourage you to take notes on the thoughts that come to you. Keep your mind open and receptive to ideas that come as you read, in talking to other business leaders and while busy doing other, unrelated things. In doing so, I believe you will begin to gain insights into your business, and implement successful strategies to act on them. These principle-grounded insights will lead you to better decision making today, so you can achieve greater business success tomorrow.

PRINCIPLES VS. LAWS

As I shared in the introduction, "principles" are concentrated truth, packaged for application to a wide variety of circumstances. According to F. Woodbridge Constant, former chairman of the physics department at Trinity College, and author of both **Fundamental Principles of Physics** and **Fundamental Laws of Physics,** a principle tells physicists how the world works in general. Principles tend not to be specific rules that can be written in mathematical terms. Rather, they are more like "guiding theories" that allow scientists to make predictions about new phenomena and develop new laws that clearly explain these phenomena.

In contrast to the guiding theories of principles, "laws" are perfectly clear. According to Woodbridge, physicists define laws with mathematical statements, which cannot be interpreted subjectively. This is why laws are considered to be more reliable than principles in clearly defining rules of nature in a way that all physicists can agree on. The key difference between a law and a principle is that laws have no exceptions.

The challenge with "principles" is that they have a tint of uncertainty, arising from their lack of clear mathematical definition. For example, the "Uncertainty Principle," in quantum physics, states that when you measure two aspects of a physical particle, such as in measuring both the position and velocity of an object, you can never know both of the aspects with perfect precision. Even though this principle does not have a mathematical form of its own, it has guided physicists to develop specific mathematical statements to apply to specific cases, such as for the position and momentum of a particle moving within a box.

Laws in physics are unbreakable, just like laws in mathematics and in nature. Take *Ohm's Law*, which states I=V/R, where "I" is current, "V" is potential difference and "R" is resistance. Because a physical law is always true, if you know two of the values in an equation, you can always calculate the third. Such laws often lead to practical applications.

Applied physics, mathematics and engineering all follow known laws in the development of new thinking, yet in business, identifying similar types of laws proves elusive. To become a law, a principle must be practical, applicable everywhere, and in any circumstance. But this is impossible in business because of the nuances involved. No matter how varied they may be all good, great, and even failing business must follow the same basic business fundamentals. You can adopt the same strategy, implement it in the exact same way, and at the same time, at two different businesses, and you will get at least two different results 100% of the time.

SELLING PROMISES

Take, for example, the concept of franchising. Every franchisor sells the promise that their formula for success will help every aspiring franchisee also become a success. Lengthy franchise agreements are signed legal contracts. The well-established franchisor consents to provide its brand, operational model and business support, in order for the franchisee to finance and run a similar business. This is in exchange for a franchise fee and an agreed-upon percentage of the franchisee's future sales.

The franchisor is offering a packaged business model built upon a track record of success. Their method of doing business is proven to produce successful results, yet every day, franchisees fail for a variety of reasons. This brief example reconfirms why strong business leaders are able to identify principles to guide us in our actions, but rarely come up with concrete "laws" for others to religiously follow to reach guaranteed success.

FRAMEWORK FOR SUCCESS

As you unlock each element of truth for your business, you must carefully examine it, in the light of both prior knowledge and emerging trends, to determine where it really fits. Ponder it, inspect it inside out, and study it from multiple vantage points—to confirm that you have not jumped to false conclusions. Your thoughtful reflection will yield deep understanding and enhance your ability to make the critical changes necessary for owning a great business.

I want to restate my primary goal in writing this book: to provide you an easy-to-follow framework that allows you to organize the truth, and unlock the secrets to owning a great business.

Discovering the unique statements of principle for your business will guide you in making better decisions. You'll soon learn that each truth you organize into a simple statement of principle will help you make decisions with confidence, even under the most confusing circumstances.

As you proceed, remember that the effort you put forth now will produce lasting dividends for your business. Always consider the long-range implications of short-range decisions.

Keep in mind that acting on the seven organizing principles for owning a great business isn't about trying to do everything at once. The strength of principles is about recognizing where you are most vulnerable, and starting there. I'm confident that as you study each of the seven principles, you'll find that some principles stand out as having more significance for your business. And those principles are a great place to begin making the most impactful changes in the way your run your business.

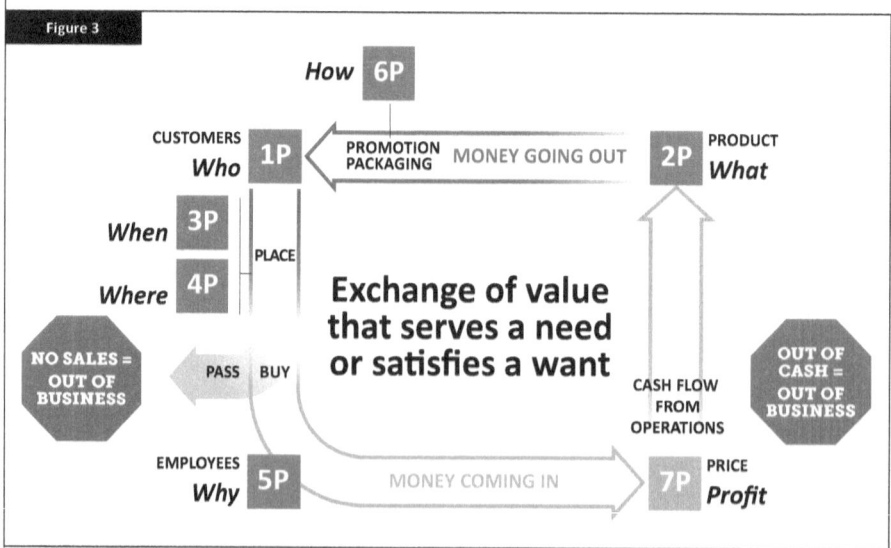

Figure 3

MODEL TO FOLLOW

You can't have a quality business book that helps you run a better business, without a concise model that shortcuts the thought process. Figure 3 is my model for the 7 Organizing Principles for Owning a Great Business. (The balance of this book lays out the logic for this framework in detail.)

On the surface, the 7-P Framework's individual elements are fairly basic, and have been discussed in many well-written business books. So, what's different about this book? I've come up with a framework that consolidates the 5W's + H with the 4 Ps of Marketing, built from my accumulated wisdom, gained from the school of hard knocks and hard work of over a quarter century in corporate employment and small business ownership. Just like you, I have also observed other small businesses make mistakes and vowed that I could do better. This formula has been born of all these experiences.

I know first-hand that answering the questions contained in the 7-P Framework requires some hard thinking. In fact, there are a few questions, particularly tied to the third principle ("when") that I have yet to answer to my satisfaction, for my own business. You may find a different one that gives you pause to think and reflect on your own situation.

GAIN INSIGHTS

I know from experience that when you and I take the time to think through the truths we encounter for our businesses, we are able to make more confident decisions. Often, our decisions are easily obscured by the shadows of a changing environment.

Wise decision making is the key to business success. Over the years, relying on this process has brought to light hidden insights about my own business, helped increase my sales and earned my company higher profits. I am confident in the process and encourage you to adopt the ideas gained here to make your business great.

CUSTOMERS/EMPLOYEE INTERSECTION

The 7-P Framework model begins with customers: the people who are buying from you based on a need or want that is fulfilled by your employees, who deliver the product or service that meets these needs or satisfies these wants.

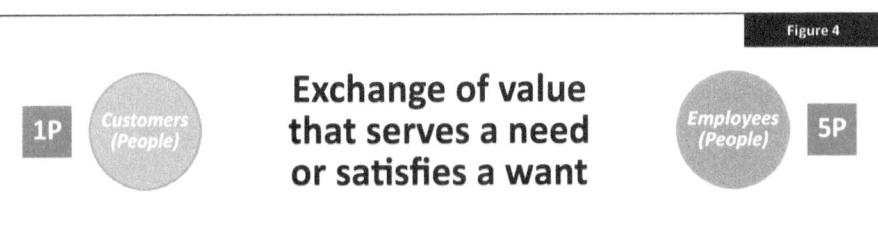

Figure 4

The success of your business ultimately comes down to whether your target customer chooses to buy, or pass, on your product or solution. If they pass, or choose not to buy from you, there is no exchange of value. If your customer does proceed to buy, or seek your services, did the transaction result in a profit or loss for your business?

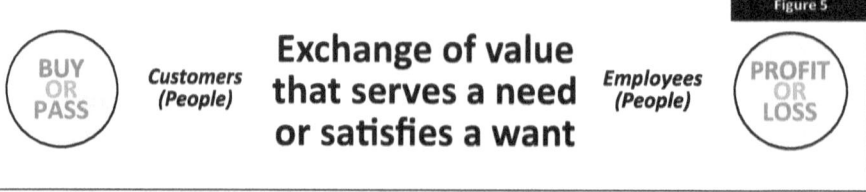

Figure 5

Defining "customers" as "step 1" in the 7-P framework is important, because the first organizing principle for doing great business involves the clear identification of your target customer. Chapter 3, beginning on page 31, walks you through the process of flushing out this first organizing principle, answering the critical who question.

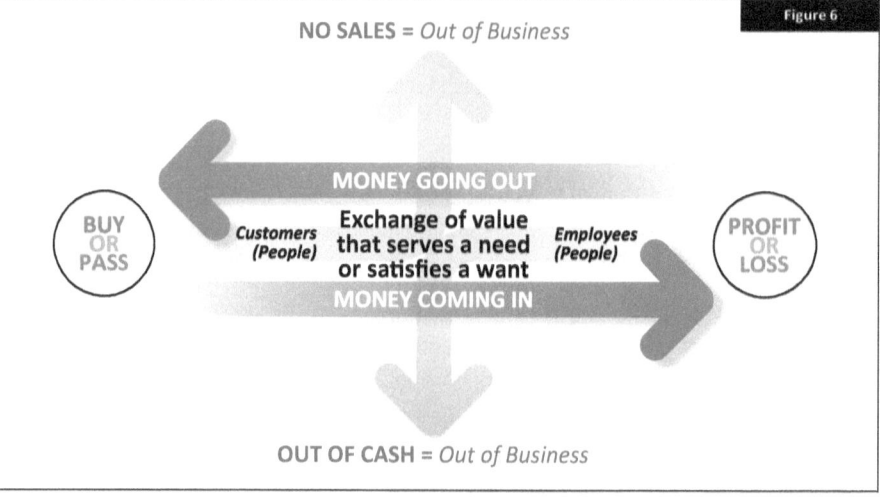

Figure 6

As you can see in Figure 6, the secondary challenge is that money coming in from a sale needs to produce a profit, or you will run out of cash to fund your business, even though you are generating sales. Running out of cash to fund your business is a "law" of business, not a principle. What amazes me is how frequently losses on a sale occur. These losses happen either because business leaders have wasted their cash flow trying to generate that sale, or because they have inefficient operations that produce losses, rather than profits, on their transactions.

PROTECT YOUR CASH FLOW

As a business owner, you need to protect your cash flow by producing profitable sales through products and services at a price people are willing to pay, while producing a profit for you. This is the "sweet spot."

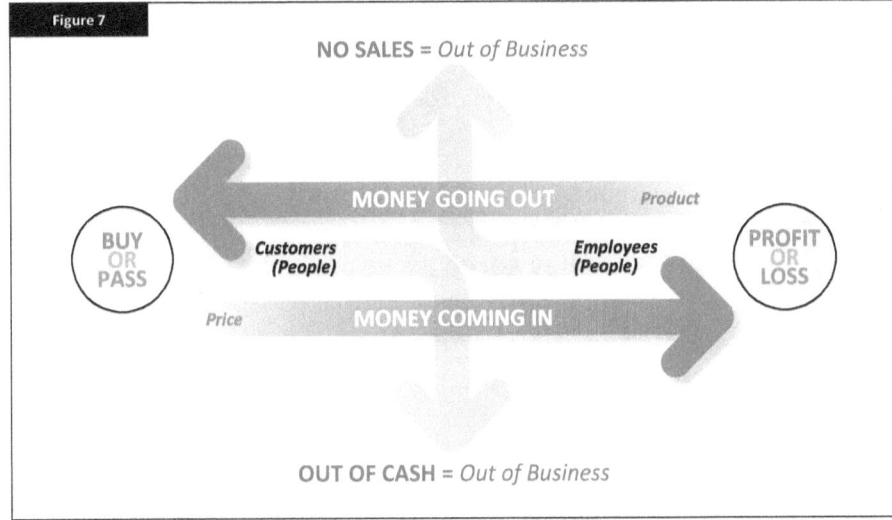

Figure 7

To run a business otherwise leads to only one conclusion: you won't have a business for long. This law is irrefutable: any exchange of value is going to originate with a business offering a product that serves a need or satisfies a want at a price that a customer is willing to pay.

So, it's essential to know the who in your business model.

2P =WHAT | PRODUCT

The second organizing principle is knowing, with precision and clarity, what problem your target customer is trying to solve. It's an essential question to answer, and one that can prevent you from going out of business!

For help in understanding and applying the principle associated with what for your business, see: Chapter 4, beginning on page 37 to develop greater clarity on why people choose to buy your products and services.

TRANSACTION ENABLERS

The transaction enablers are place, promotion, and packaging. These three Ps from the marketing mix is how you get your target customer to know you exist. This is how you help them make an informed decision to buy or not to buy at the price you are charging. You can't own a great business if you aren't meeting your daily, weekly and monthly transaction goals.

I like to look at transactions per day and average dollar value per transaction. It's important to look at both because a high transaction volume can be deceptive. You and your employees can be busy processing a growing volume of orders, but actually be losing ground because your new sales are lowering your average transaction value.

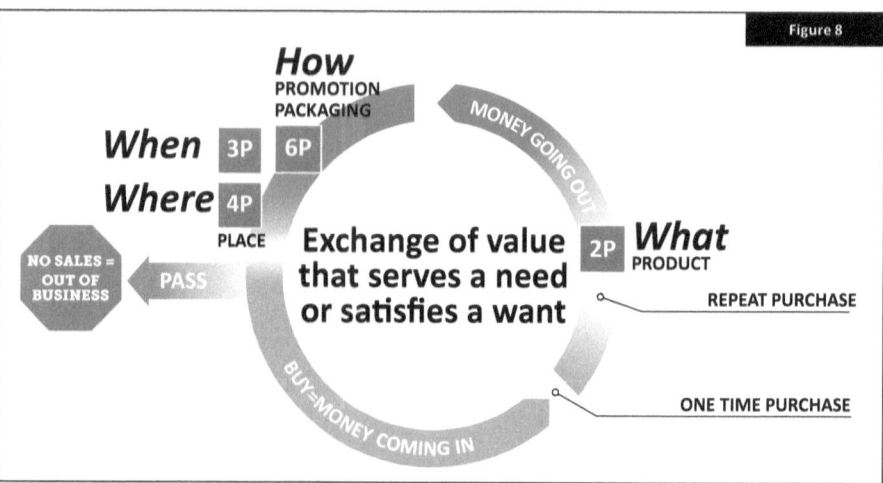

Your revenue must cover your costs. If you aren't careful in your management of your transaction enablers you can find yourself spending a lot of money. You will think you are working hard in a growing business and yet be losing money. You cannot be profitable if your expenses tied to your growth are growing at a faster pace than the revenue being generated. This is a hard lesson we all learn at one time or another.

3P = WHEN + 4P = WHERE | PLACE

There are two organizing principles associated with "place." The first involves when your customer will most likely need your help, and the second concerns where they will choose to transact their business.

In the 21st Century, this is not such a simple question to answer. Many of you reading this and preparing to put the principles into action, do not run brick and mortar stores.

TIME AND TECHNOLOGY

We live in a global economy, which functions at all hours of the day, in every time zone on the map. Before the industrial revolution, "shift-work" did not exist. As a member of the work force, you got up with the cows and went to sleep with the cows, or, more likely, worked from dawn until dusk. There were no all-night fast food restaurants, 24/7 emergency rooms or phone banks located in Mumbai, but serving rural America.

The question of when business was transacted was answered very simply: when it was possible to do so. Virtually every barrier of time and geography has been eliminated in the new economy.

Similarly, the question of where has changed dramatically, particularly due to the rise of Internet-based sales and other business opportunities.

EXAMPLE: FOOD

Looking at a simple example: buying groceries. While many people enjoy the ages-old experience of buying produce at a farmer's market, there are literally a dozen other options for today's consumers. Perhaps you order by phone or online, and have your groceries delivered to your door. Some of our neighbors purchase from a food co-op, which requires active involvement and financial participation. Others believe in ordering in bulk from a mail-order company; or belonging to a CSA (Community-Supported Agriculture) outlet, which delivers to a central location, from which you pick up your pre-boxed order.

So many choices! And every one of these business models needs to be profitable, or at least sustainable or revenue-neutral, to survive. So, as part of your investigation into discovering the truth about your business, ask yourself, what options for when and where are you offering?

For a great deal more guidance on understanding and applying the third organizing principle, see: Chapter, 5, beginning on page 47; and for more on following the fourth organizing principle, where, see: Chapter 6, beginning on page 57. Reading through both of these chapters will help you to avoid making a costly "fatal flaw" in owning a great business.

5P = WHY | PEOPLE

The fifth organizing principle involves why, which is shorthand for how do I create value for my customer? It's akin to your "customer value proposition." To clearly grasp the fifth principle, you will need to ask yourself the necessary questions that allow you to understand the leadership structure, company culture, and strategic style of your business.

Ultimately, your employees need to clearly understand all the ways in which they create value for your customers in the work that they do.

> **Ultimately, your employees need to clearly understand all the ways in which they create value for your customers...**

If you fail to answer the why question, you'll expose yourself to the most commonly stated reason for businesses to fail, and that is, running out of cash. Does that sound like an old refrain? It is the number one reason for most businesses to fail. You are head and shoulders above them, just by getting a handle on your cash flow.

The primary challenge of business is cash flow: you have to spend cash to generate sales. You may have a lot of money going out, aimed at convincing your target customer to buy from you. And if your marketing strategy is effective, you will have sales coming in to more than cover this investment. But if you fail to produce sales, you will lose your business as you run out of cash. Understanding the why of your business model is crucial.

These are tricky questions to ask, and it may take some digging to come up with the answers. You'll learn much more about the fifth organizing principle, the why, later on, in Chapter 7, beginning on page 57.

Now, let's review what we've learned so far:
1. *You have to know who your customer is,*
2. *What problem they are trying to solve,*
3. *When they are most likely to need your help, and*
4. *Where they prefer to transact business.*

Once you know these "business basics," you can then define why they should value what your business offers. Gaining all of these insights, early on in your business, will help you align your company culture and ultimately your employees' actions in delivering value to your customers.

6P = HOW | PROMOTION + PACKAGING

After you have defined the why for your employees, from thoroughly working with Chapter 7, you will then be ready to move on to the sixth organizing principle. This principle involves helping your customers understand how they should value what you do by purchasing products and services from you at a price that earns your business a profit.

How do you demonstrate value to your customer? The answer lies in how you promote and package your products and services. For in-depth details on promotion and packaging, see: Chapter 8, beginning on page 81.

SELECT A STRATEGY

I also want to use the 7-P Framework to help you avoid the "seven fatal flaws" in business. This easy-to-comprehend framework will help you think through the core elements of your business. You will be glad you took the time to do this.

...your business will likely never have the resources to endlessly pursue different business strategies...

The payoff will be much more than just money. You will realize greater satisfaction from your hard work as you build and sustain a great and long lasting business.

It requires a lot of personal effort to gain and apply the necessary knowledge that makes up the 7-P Framework. And let's face it; your business will likely never have the resources to endlessly pursue different business strategies. So, you must carefully select those few vital areas on which to focus your time, energy, and resources.

Make a definite choice to follow this framework and commit to practicing it consistently for one full year. You can do it. I have confidence in you.

I know first-hand that running an ongoing business, while trying to gain new insights and knowledge, requires extraordinary personal effort, particularly when your desire is to build a lasting business.

Application of the information organizing power of the 5 W's + H coupled with the 4 Ps of marketing to the large and small business decisions you make every day will greatly improve your probability of success. This process will accelerate your move toward owning a great business.

7P = PROFIT | PRICE

Even when you take the time to apply many of the principles you've learned about in this book, you still face the ultimate problem: to remain a viable business, you must continue to earn a profit.

The seventh principle associated with profitability is partnered with "price." Establishing the correct price-point for your products and services, that "sweet spot," is a learned art.

ALWAYS REMEMBER THE CASH FLOW

I will walk you through the critical price considerations you need to consider, in order to better ensure that your business generates profits, not losses. While the process is easy, it is not necessarily simple. You will find if you make a commitment to this formula it will soon become a habit. Just like all the other things in life. Do it often enough, and it becomes automatic action.

> *...to remain a viable business, you must continue to earn a profit...*

I hope that after familiarizing yourself with the 7-P Framework at an "executive summary" level, you'll begin to develop your own new thoughts, observations and insights about your business.

Thoughtful use of the framework presented in *Owning a GREAT Business: 7 organizing PRINCIPLES: so yours is one of them!* will position you to make a significant difference in the lives of your customers and employees.

Take the time now to carefully think through the 7-P Framework. Discover the truths that lead you to make great decisions and take effective actions. What you incorporate will help you achieve your goal of owning a great business. Your future depends on it. Not only your future, but also the livelihoods of your family and loved ones as well as your employees and their loved ones are counting on your success.

Your community is counting on your success to build roads, schools, and parks and bring visitors to your site or store. It's a big responsibility.

For more on understanding the relationship between price and profit, see Chapter 9, beginning on page 91

CHAPTER THREE
1st ORGANIZING PRINCIPLE: WHO?
Target Customer

You can't build a great company until you know who is most likely to benefit from the products or services you offer, your customer. This is ultimately who you are building your company for, the very reason for its existence.

Can you truly articulate all of the decisions your customers must make in choosing to purchase from you, and not your competitor? Knowing their purchasing decision criteria allows you to efficiently organize your resources, and to deliver the best products and services to your customers at a profit.

MUST KNOW YOUR CUSTOMER

Let's take a look at what might happen if you don't know your customer well? If I blindfolded you and asked you to cross over the 405 freeway in California, that connects Orange County and Los Angeles, at rush hour, would you do it? Of course not, you are a smart and talented individual who is called an entrepreneur for a reason.

Trying to run a business without a clear and precise understanding of your customer base is like crossing the 405, with a blindfold on...

Trying to run a business without a clear and precise understanding of your customer base is like crossing the 405, with a blindfold on, in rush-hour traffic. It's a recipe for disaster for you and the motorists fighting to avoid running you over.

RECIPE FOR SUCCESS

You can prevent a "recipe for disaster" in business by identifying your target customers—those who are easiest to work with and who will allow you to profit from the purchase they make with you.

You begin building a great business when you know, with precision, who will benefit most from the products and services you offer. Many well-intentioned marketing professionals get stuck on narrowly-identifying the demographics and psychographics of the "ideal" customer.

From my perspective and experience, these factors and statistics don't matter if your customers are difficult to work with and if you don't make a profit when they purchase from your business. Small businesses live and die on the strength of their reciprocal relationships: your target customers need you to make money; otherwise, you'll go out of business and be unable to continue to provide the goods and services they need.

APRICOTS OR APPLES

The most basic way to identify your target customer is to ask yourself this simple question: who benefits most from your product? It has been said that every business is like a tree. No one can pick apricots from apple trees.

If you grow only apple trees, those customers looking for apricots will never buy from you. They will never be your target customers, because they only want to buy apricots, not apples. So, if you want to target apricot-loving customers, you will have to plant apricot trees in your orchard. (And you may want to evaluate whether you should continue to grow, harvest, and sell apples...)

How you serve the needs or satisfy the wants of your customers, while earning a profit, is the core definition of your business. The people you identify who will benefit most from what you do comprises your target customer base. What makes these particular customers easy to serve? It's a critical question to answer, and you can begin to refine your target customer search by asking the following key questions:

KEY QUESTIONS
1. *What does your target customer do? (behavior)*
2. *How often, and at what volume, does the behavior occur? (frequency/quantity)*
3. *Where, or in what factors, does the customer find value? (motivation)*

BROAD OR NARROW BASE

While articulating the answers to these questions helps identify your target customer, I've found that the best way to define who begins with knowing, with certainty, the breadth of your product's appeal.

Do you have a broad user base, allowing many different types of customers to benefit from what you do, or do you have a narrow customer base, where only a small group of users will express interest in your product?

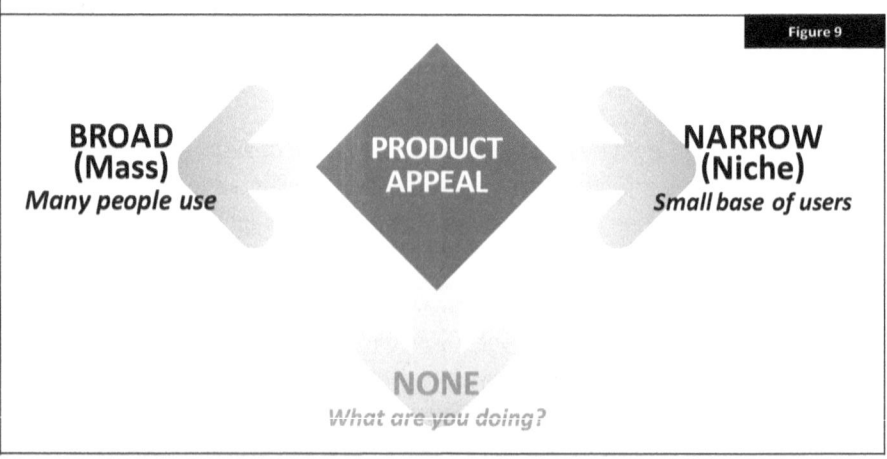

At PPG, I worked in the Coil Coating division, where we had less than fifty possible customers across the United States. We knew every one of our potential customers, because we only sold to coil coaters—a narrow base of users, indeed. Our problem wasn't in defining the who; it was in several different business flaws that we'll look at later in this book.

At Veterinary Pet Insurance, we could have promoted our business to more than 60% of U.S. households who have at least one pet. If you are reading this book and you don't have a pet at home, you weren't our target customer. Not having a pet was of no use in focusing in on our target customer base, because it wasn't relevant.

While most marketing consultants will push you to define your target customer, they sometimes fail to stress the importance of first determining whether your business serves a broad or narrow customer base.

When you have a product with narrow appeal, defining your target customer with precision and clarity is your key organizing principle. For example, at VPI, less than 1% of the pet-owning population had pet insurance. Since VPI's start-up in 1987, over fifty pet health insurance companies have come and gone. Those who went out of business made a critical mistake: while they saw the enormity of the large, untapped market of pet owners as their potential customer base, they failed to clearly and precisely identify who their target customers were, beyond those who simply owned a pet.

WHO NEEDS YOU?

The marketing problem at VPI was more clearly defined: we needed to figure out which of the forty-three million dog owners and thirty-seven million cat owners were interested in pet health insurance. We had a limited marketing budget, so we couldn't promote our business to every pet owner. This is more often the case in every business.

Before I came to VPI, they had failed to invest in quality market research relative to defining their ideal customer base. Sales came to VPI via the "hope" method, rather than strategy. By conducting thorough customer research, we were able to clearly define our best target customers, and as a result, we were able to grow our policyholder base by targeting customers more effectively.

We gave our best target customers the label of "pet parents," because they considered their pets to be members of their family. This was their most important defining characteristic. "Pet parents" were, by far, the most likely pet owners to purchase pet health insurance. (For those who are interested, the best way to recognize "pet parents" is by the pictures on their desks and the screen background photos on their phones. If you see a picture of a dog or cat without a human, you are talking to a pet parent.)

TARGET CUSTOMER

At Design Dynamics, we appeal to a broad base of customers. Our best customers are those who have something important to say, in a big way. If they don't have anything important to say about their business, they don't need us, and we're not interested in selling people graphics or signage that they don't need or want. It doesn't fit our business model, and they would not be our target customers.

I have spent a lot of time trying to define our target customer, because it's the accepted foundation of all great marketing. In doing then revisiting this fundamental marketing exercise for my business, I came to appreciate that knowing the who for your business has different levels of importance, based on whether your product satisfies a want or a need, and whether your business has a broad or narrow customer base.

You will want to determine your customer base. Are they Apricots or Apples? Is your base broad or narrow? How do you appeal to them so they will buy your product?

NARROW BASE IN NICHES

Businesses that appeal to a narrow customer base need to define the who with precision. Businesses that start from a particular hobby, and that cater to people who share that hobby, tend to have a narrow customer base. If this is you, the organizing principles associated with who is your most important "W." This is otherwise known as "niche marketing."

One of our more rapidly growing customers is Cousins Tackle. When you buy a Cousin's Rod, you're buying nothing less than quality workmanship. Cousins Tackle makes one of the finest fishing rods you can buy anywhere in the world. Their rod blanks are made, assembled, and shipped all over the world, from their Huntington Beach, California, factory. Our contribution is the logo decal prominent on each rod.

The target customers for Cousins Tackle are fishermen and women who want only the highest-quality components in their fishing rod, so they can catch more fish. Those who don't fish are not their target, nor is the fisherman who would buy a rod at WalMart. As a result, they serve a narrower market than the popular brand, Zebco. What I appreciate about our friends at Cousins Tackle is that they understand this "truth," and, as a result, their business has been growing rapidly for the last three years.

TOO MANY CUSTOMERS

If your business already has too many customers, then I would encourage you to stop reading and return this book while you can still get your money back. Having too many customers would be a wonderful problem to have.

Yet that isn't the problem this book is intended to solve, because I have yet to meet a small business owner who worried about having too many quality customers!

Consider the TV show Law & Order (NBC, 1990-2010), which was on the air for twenty years, airing 456 episodes. It became the third-longest-running scripted TV series of all time, and it spun-off three successful, and two unsuccessful, additional series.

Dick Wolf, the creator of the show, consistently followed the same formula for each episode: It was usually adapted from current headlines, and the theme was shown from two separate vantage points. The first half of the show concentrated on the investigation of the crime by the police, and then the second half followed the prosecution of the criminals in court.

FOLLOW THE FORMULA

The who is extremely important in TV writing, particularly in crime dramas. Every crime in any crime drama has at least two people of utmost importance: the victim and the criminal. In Law and Order, these two were expertly balanced. The writers shaped each of these character's wants, desires and ambitions in order to create an effective and compelling episode week after week.

WHO KNOWS, LIKES, & TRUSTS YOU

The writers have to be intimately aware of another who, as well: their audience. The details and dynamics of the characters they create need to continue to attract their audience every week. If TV writers lose focus or stop understanding what their audience wants, the series will lose its viewership.

The twenty-year success of Law & Order, along with the fact that it's still a top moneymaker in syndication, is evidence of this mastery of, and power in, fully understanding the who.

Knowing the who takes time. It is time well spent. It requires a lot of hard thinking to clearly and precisely define the type of customer who is motivated to buy from you. Getting the who right goes a very long way in owning a great business, because you will have identified the concentrated truths about your customers, packaged for application to a wide variety of decisions you need to make and actions you will want to take.

This initial piece of the formula is key, because everything else in the 7-P Framework will follow from your answer to who, particularly for those who have products that appeal to a narrow audience. If your product appeal is broad, then the next two "W's" are even more important to your success than having a perfect definition of who. Let's see how this applies

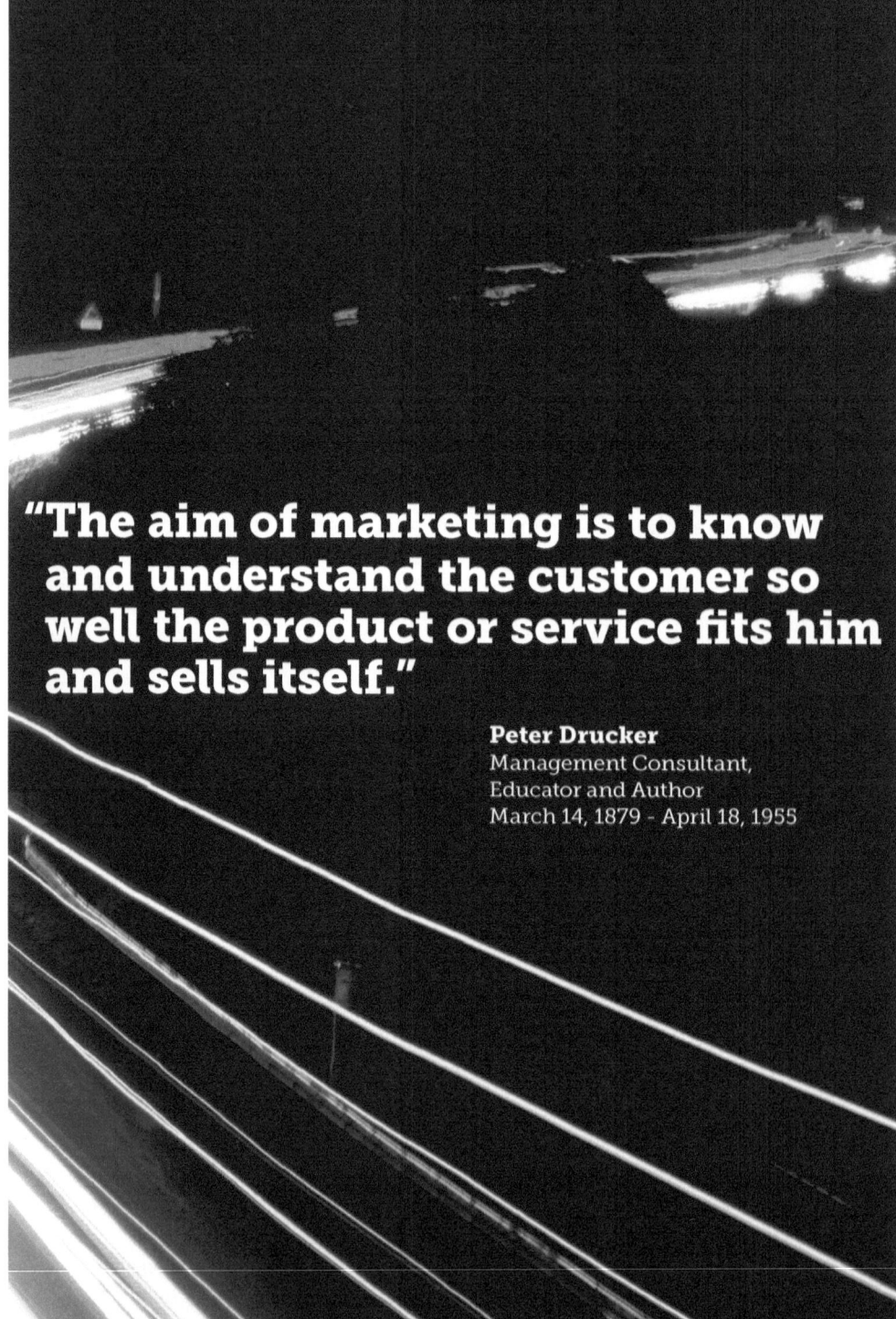

CHAPTER FOUR

2nd ORGANIZING PRINCIPLE: WHAT?
Product

Companies fail when they don't truly understand what features consumers value, how much they are willing to pay for those features, and what consumers and other businesses are willing to trade in order to get what they each value.

PROBLEM-SOLUTION

The key question is: What problem is the person buying from you trying to solve? As a business owner, you must be able to answer this question, or risk losing the sale. When you help people buy the things they need and provide products they value, you will be successful. Your business will be the one they tell their friends about, and word-of-mouth is the best form of advertising.

So, knowing what problem your customer is trying to solve is the key to providing products and services for which your customers will pay a fair market price. Not knowing how much specific product features are valued means you are at risk for "under-selling" your product.

Answering the what question—identifying the features your customers' value most—enables you to charge a premium price for what you do, with confidence.

This is particularly true when your understanding of the application of your product or service leads the consumer to finding your solution to their problem before they are even aware they have a problem. They may just be annoyed by aching feet or a garage door that doesn't close correctly and not think about a solution or that things could be any other way. Until you help them understand that they no longer have to be annoyed or irritated they will go blindly along cursing the door and limping on their sore feet.

Consider the reason that people buy drill bits: to drill holes. It isn't even the hole they are seeking. It is the cupboard they are hanging in the kitchen. What they really want is to be able to store stuff in a cupboard. In order to hang the cupboard that stores the stuff, the hole has to be drilled. In order to drill the hole, they need the correct size bit. Understanding this need flow is how you successfully shape your marketing mix decisions involving price, promotion, place and packaging.

ALREADY DEFINED PRODUCTS

Many business leaders reading this book are working with products that are already defined; the resources in your business are already dedicated to making your product, and delivering your services.

The hard work your company does revolves around the product you are already producing and selling—and this book will help you unlock the truths for your business that will help you sell even more of the products you already produce and deliver.

BUSINESS INNOVATIONS

This book is also for those who are wrestling with designing or launching a new product. Before investing your life savings in a new business venture, I would encourage you to learn the pitfalls to avoid, and the formula to follow for success.

In addition to learning from *Owning a GREAT Business: 7 Organizing PRINCIPLES So Yours is One of Them!* I would encourage you to seek guidance from one of the many books on business innovation.

BENEFITS NOT FEATURES

How do you, as a business owner, begin to define the what for your customer? Focus on the benefit your customer derives, not on the tangible features of the product.

To appreciate this fundamental point, let's go back to the drill bit example. It's the holes the bit drills that initiate the purchase, not the bit itself. A product's potential is shaped by the problem it solves. The key take-away for unlocking this principle is talking to your customers, in order to understand what problems your products or services help them solve. Your goal is to first identify what is the equivalent to the "hole" for them, and then come up with the perfect "drill bit."

> *A product's potential is shaped by the problem it solves.*

The concept of benefits and features are often confusing for many in business. A simple trick is to state something about your product and then ask "So that...." the drill bit can make medium size holes so that medium size screws can easily be put in.

In our community there are many box hardware stores, just as there are where you live. However, every year a small business owned hardware store is chosen number 1. The reason, the employees not only sell you the drill, but also teach you how to use it for many things you may not have thought of before buying.

Why did your customer make the decision to buy from you? What problem were you able to solve for them? Gathering the information necessary to answer these questions is one of the best ways to ensure that your business solves its customers' needs better, and differently, than anyone else (and for you to make more money in the process).

In fact, this formula is the key to product success. If you fail to do this important work, you'll be seen as just another "me too" business. If you only provide the product and not solve the problem the consumer's decision is all about finding the lowest price for the product or service. There is no incentive to choose your business over your competitor's.

> *If you only provide the product and not solve the problem the consumer's decision is all about finding the lowest price for the product or service.*

Before talking with your best customers, it's important for you to understand whether you think your customers view your product as new and innovative, or existing and proven.

Four of the six Ps from the expanded marketing mix can help you connect with your target customer, by focusing on those customers who can benefit most from what you have to offer. This is shown below:

Figure 10

● PROMOTION

For example, if your target customer sees your product as brand new, your best marketing option is promotion. Your goal is to create visually compelling graphics illustrating the reasons why people should try your product.

Why visually compelling? Because people are most likely to act on what they "see," in comparison to what they might taste, touch, hear and smell. 80% of the population are visual and respond to those clues they can see.

Now, more than ever, it's a highly visual world. Advertisers know this, and capitalize on it, big time.

● PACKAGING

If people don't see your product as "brand new," yet you have improved your product so that it offers a better value, your optimum marketing lever is new packaging.

Packaging is included in the expanded 6 Ps marketing mix because of its important role in attracting attention, as well as imparting essential or additional product specific information to help trigger purchasing decisions.

● PLACE

If your consumer base is narrow, and product is scarce or hard to get, you have to show them where to go to buy it. "Place" is the location of the market, and includes the means of distribution used in reaching it. If you want more people to buy your product, you'll need to focus on generating continuous traffic to the "place" your target prefers to transact business. Where you want to sell your product is irrelevant. For more on the where principle and what you can do about place considerations, see Chapter 6, beginning on page 57.

● PRICE

If your product or service is widely available and relatively easy to access, you're in the most difficult of competitive situations. In this situation, more often than not it's going to come down to price or easy access to the product if the place is right.

Your strategy here is to find creative ways to show the value of buying from your business over your competitor's, or, you can relentlessly trim your operation for efficiency so that you can provide your product at a lower cost. To learn what is required for a winning strategic style, see Chapter 7, beginning on page 69.

PRODUCT DEVELOPMENT

Another common cause of business failure is "product complacency" by the business owner and his or her employees. Your product may be the best thing out there today, yet that doesn't mean it will be great tomorrow. You can sit on your thumbs and do nothing in terms of innovation, or take the risk of speaking with your best customers to learn information that might initiate changes in your product, or your marketing strategies.

> *Your product may be the best thing out there today, yet that doesn't mean it will be great tomorrow.*

As you learn what your best customers are saying about your product, keep an open mind, and carefully consider what it is you need to do better to create and market products that your customers value and want to buy. The world is a dynamic place. As a result, there will always be opportunities to do, and be, better in any business.

No product is static, and new ways of doing things will always replace the old. Continuously improving your products through adding new features and benefits, or more efficient production and distribution to keep costs down, is another key organizing principle which can create value for your customers, and turn into profits for you.

NEW AND IMPROVED

Your **what** can become a "fatal flaw" if you become complacent in the belief that your product is fine just the way it is. Or, there may be key people in your organization that will not accept change. I personally love and welcome change; yet I know that most people hate it. This is because change isn't easy—it requires work.

Charles Darwin observed, "It is not the strongest of species that survive, nor the most intelligent,

> *"What" can become a "fatal flaw" if you become complacent in the belief that your product is fine just the way it is...*

but the most responsive to change." And how do we respond to change? By adaptation. It's a process, and it won't happen overnight.

Consider the Kodak Company, and what happened as they opted to sideline their digital camera technology. At one time, Kodak was one of America's great companies, competing on fronts well beyond their photography product lines. Looking back, it's a little hard to believe, but Kodak was actually the first to develop digital technology for cameras, and for what would ultimately become the cell phone.

COULDA, WOULDA, SHOULDA

Unfortunately, they squandered the opportunities they created through their R&D, and failed to take the technology and run with it. Senior executives made the fatal decision to "sit" on these new developments in order to protect their core business; rather than taking the leap, they viewed the new technology as a "threat" to their existing film products.

If they had made different business decisions, Kodak could have become the Apple, Google, or even Facebook of today. Change and adaptation are necessary to the process of evolution, whether in nature or in business. Those who don't make the necessary changes will not survive and prosper.

Blockbuster Video is another example: When was the last time you rented a video from Blockbuster? These days you can't even locate their stores, with the colorful blue awnings. But in its prime, Blockbuster was blamed for killing off small independent video rental stores. They used their size and distribution power to create stores which had multiple copies of the high-demand movies. Consumers stopped going to smaller independent video rental stores, because they were often out of the movies they wanted to see. It was so much easier to go to Blockbuster—which always had just the movies they were looking for.

THE WORLD IS NOT STATIC

Soon, Netflix came along and turned the entertainment industry on its head. Before Netflix, home video rentals were King, and Blockbuster Video ruled on high. Blockbuster's leadership believed they were the 800-pound gorilla in home entertainment, and they were blind to the dramatic shift that was coming.

Here's something you might not know: Blockbuster was given the option to purchase the budding Netflix company in the early 2000s, for fifty million dollars—but, they opted not to. I don't know how much this decision was debated by the Blockbuster board of directors and senior management, but what I do know is that this decision ultimately led to the company's destruction. Netflix went on to grow beyond anybody's expectations, eventually changing their video rental delivery model to include on-demand content, and now, even Netflix-produced original series. And Blockbuster, the giant gorilla in home entertainment, went out of business.

What's so sad about Kodak and Blockbuster is that they were truly industry leaders, and benchmarks against which many businesses measured themselves. Benchmarking is a widely accepted "best practice" for learning how well your products and business are performing. While benchmarking the competition has some value, it too-often becomes the ceiling, and creates a false sense of security.

BE READY TO MOVE FORWARD

Why do you need to talk to your customers, particularly when your benchmark results show you are doing better than your peers? Because failing to talk with your customers prevents you from learning what they value in your product. It prevents you from identifying the key changes you need to make to keep your business thriving.

> *...failing to talk with your customers prevents you from learning what they value in your product.*

Truly, the longer I'm in business, the less interested I am in benchmarking myself against my competition. I prefer talking with my best customers to appreciate what it is they value in our products and us.

Companies who rely primarily on benchmarking to learn what others are doing more often than not end up being copycats. This floods the field and forces the consumer to buy solely on price, because these businesses have failed to offer substantive reasons to choose one business over another.

Yes, you need to be aware of your competition, but need to make business decisions on the best information available, which comes from knowing your customers well, and meeting their needs in better and different ways.

FOLLOWER OR INNOVATOR

Ask yourself this hard question, with honesty: "Am I a follower or an innovator?" If you're a follower, even a quick and efficient follower, then your key to success is in product availability. Your challenge is that over time, you will begin to lose customers to the business that is first to market the innovations their customers' value, and will pay a premium to obtain.

Another example that illustrates the importance of knowing what the customer values in a product involves Keurig. Consider how the shares for Keurig Green Mountain (GMCR) rebounded on May 8, 2015, as investors digested the company's apology.

During a conference call two days earlier, CEO Brian Kelley acknowledged that his company had made a key mistake with their new line of single-coffee cup brewing systems: The new brewers were designed to prevent consumers from using "non-Keurig-approved K-Cups." These new K-Cups featured bar codes that triggered the Keurig machine to brew the coffee, but they also prevented third parties from selling their own profitable coffee-pods. As part of this product change, the company had also stopped production of the "My K-Cup pods" that allowed consumers to use whatever coffee grounds they wanted, which often cost less than the Keurig brand locked-down versions.

Because this decision did not honor what the customers valued, it wasn't in the best interest of their consumers, or ultimately, the Keurig Company. Sales of the new brewing systems plunged 23%, as consumers voted against the proprietary coffee system with their wallets. And this led to the apology by Keurig, and a reversal of the changes to the previous product. Lesson learned, but an expensive lesson.

What impresses me about this story is the CEO actually stood up and owned the decision to change the Keurig product. He didn't blame the weather, or the economy, or the government. He was accountable. "We were wrong. 'We missed, is the easiest way to say it. We underestimated the passion the consumer had for this," Kelley said in the conference call he made with Keurig investors.

In bringing back the universal "My K-Cups," the CEO acknowledged, "It was a nice convenience for a lot of our very, very, loyal and heavy users. They didn't use it frequently, but they used it. And importantly, it gave them the ability to brew any brand they wanted," Kelley said. "We shouldn't have taken it away. We did. And we're bringing it back."

KNOWLEDGE IS KING

Knowing everything you can about your loyal customers and heavy users is important to your business success. Intelligence gathering is worthless if you don't know what problem these customers are trying to solve with their purchase. The most personally satisfying business I do is helping people buy the things they need—and the best way to help people buy the things they need is by knowing what problem they are trying to solve.

> *...the best way to help people buy the things they need is by knowing what problem they are trying to solve*

Then you can focus on communicating, in simple terms, all the ways in which your product is the perfect solution.

One of my favorite television shows from the 1990's was JAG. JAG is the U.S. military acronym for Judge Advocate General, and it became well known through this legal-drama television show, featuring a distinct U.S. Navy theme.

From a business standpoint, the what for JAG was originally perceived as a "Top Gun" meets "A Few Good Men" hybrid series. Unfortunately, this show didn't get off to a strong start, with NBC canceling the show after finishing 79th in the ratings. While NBC lacked confidence in JAG, rival network CBS picked up the series as a 1997 midseason replacement. JAG climbed in the ratings and aired for nine additional seasons. In total, 227 episodes were produced, over ten seasons.

WINNERS HAVE STAYING POWER

A winning "product" not only has staying power, but it also becomes the catalyst for new products that have the potential to outperform them. For example, while JAG aired for ten seasons, it spawned the hit series NCIS, which helped propel CBS to the number one network on TV, which in turn led to NCIS: Los Angeles and NCIS: New Orleans. To appreciate just how successful NCIS became, six years after JAG had gone off the air, NCIS was voted America's favorite television show. The series finished its tenth season as the most-watched television series in the U.S., during the 2012–13 TV season, and in May 2015, NCIS was renewed through 2018 by CBS!

NBC had the foresight to buy JAG initially, but it lacked the vision to see it through to success. While CBS saw its potential, and as a result of this business decision, they were able to earn a healthy profit over the nine years of JAG and the subsequent thirteen years and counting out of NCIS—all because they made the decision to give JAG another try.

GREAT BUSINESS IN A NUTSHELL

Doing great business begins with first knowing who your customer is, and second, clearly understanding what problem they are trying to solve. After you have unlocked the concentrated truths around who and what, and have applied these truths to building your business, you'll need to accurately define when your customers are most likely to need your help.

> ...*great business begins with first knowing who your customer is*...

"The best way to predict the future is to create it."
ABRAHAM LINCOLN

CHAPTER FIVE

3rd ORGANIZING PRINCIPLE: WHEN?
Place: Part One

Proceeding in business without knowing when your target will need or want your products or services is one of the surest ways to waste your marketing investments. This is because, at any given time, only a few of your target customers will need or want what you're offering.

TIMING IS EVERYTHING

When people aren't in the mindset to need or want what your business produces, they will fail to see your promotions. The money you're investing in marketing your business isn't being seen, because the people you're trying to influence aren't looking for or thinking about, what you're offering.

Think about the last time you were in the market for a new car. During this period, your eye may have been drawn to every new model you spotted on the road, in your favorite magazine, or on TV.

Prior to this, you were more likely to have tuned out all of the car ads on TV, or on your favorite radio station; your eye probably sailed right past the signage of the car dealerships along your route to work. But then, as your interest in a new car grew, you began paying attention to the advertising as you started shopping around. And the more you shopped, the more you narrowed you're list of features that you were looking for in your new car—otherwise known as your make and model "consideration set."

As you began to focus in on the type of car you were leaning toward, the more you noticed how many people were driving the car you were considering. Then you also started to notice how many people are driving the precise color of car you were thinking of parking in your garage.

YOU ONLY HOOK THE HUNGRY FISH

Unless you're selling exclusively to impulse buyers, your success will depend on your ability to sell to inquiring minds. As illustrated in the above scenario, your mind never goes through the process of narrowing down the choices in a new car if you aren't in the market for one.

Your mind needs the right stimulation before it can respond. The space between a stimulus and a response is where our perception is formed, and where a choice is made. Without the intrusion of a new and compelling need or want, there is no choice to be made.

The entering of new knowledge allows us to form a perception of value; and without it, there will be no choice. Always promote your business in ways that help the customer make an informed choice, based on a clear perception of value.

PERCEPTION MATTERS
- **If the customer sees value = they will buy.** People are best able to see the value when they have a pressing need.
- **IF THE CUSTOMER Questions value = THEY WILL think about it, AT BEST.** This is particularly true when the need is not pressing.
- **IF THE CUSTOMER SEES No value = THEY WILL ignore, or pass ON YOUR BUSINESS.**

RIGHT TIME VS. WRONG TIME

One of my trusted advisors in marketing is Tom Becker. Tom shared a story of working for a tire company that marketed to NASCAR fans. One of their more expensive marketing campaigns was based on interacting with NASCAR fans at the racetrack, during the actual race. Gee...what could possibly be wrong with this approach—promoting tires to passionate racing fans that also, by the way, drive cars?

NASCAR fans are known for being some of the most engaged fans on the planet. They love their sport, and they spend boatloads of money at the racetrack. They wear headsets so they can tune into their favorite team's crew chatter. They are aware and knowledgeable, with an intense affinity for the sport. All true. But the last thing they would want to do, while watching a live race, is to be interrupted by marketing rep for tires.

The next time you're at a NASCAR race, or at any race for that matter, I challenge you to find someone driving home with four new tires in their backseat. It's just not going to happen.

Tom worked for Goodyear, a solid company, but in that campaign, they chose the wrong time to promote their tires. The right time was in the days and weeks leading up to the race, not at the track on race day. The place to promote Goodyear tires was at the local tire dealers within the geographic area of each race venue. Race coming up at Bristol? Run the add two to three weeks before the race.

SOLUTION DEFINES THE PRODUCT

With the right signage, such as the products we create at Design Dynamics, we could have zeroed in on the important things they wanted race fans to know about their tires, and produced their promotional campaign.

Imagine yourself at your favorite sporting event. If you live in the LA/Orange County area, you're likely to root for the Rams, Kings, Ducks, Lakers, Clippers, Angels, Dodgers, USC or UCLA. Now, envision yourself at their next game, having your ear talked off by some pushy sales guy. What a bad taste this would leave in your mouth, because you're not stupid. You know they don't "get you," or your values, and as a result, you wouldn't choose to do business with them. They are trying to sell you a product that you may or not value. The mistake is they are doing so while you're trying to enjoy watching a game with your favorite team. They are spending a lot of money to be there yet they don't get you, and they aren't likely to get your business.

While a product is defined by the problem it solves, it is most strategically identified by when the problem needs to be solved. We've all heard the saying, "timing is everything." And it's true. People will most often make a purchase when they need to solve a problem. Your job is to be sure they are aware they even have a problem.

Figure 11

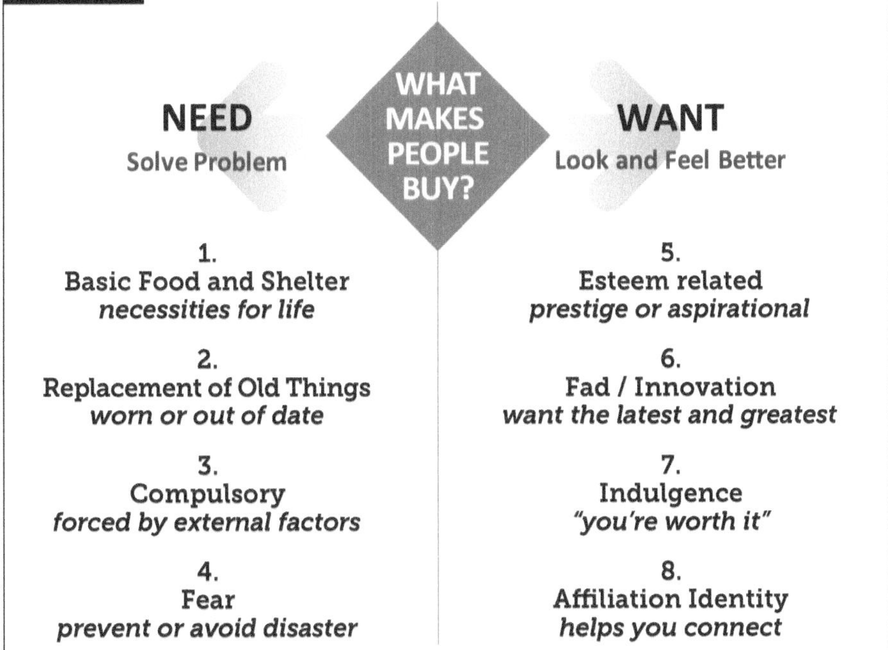

WHAT MAKES PEOPLE BUY?

NEED — Solve Problem

1. **Basic Food and Shelter** — *necessities for life*
2. **Replacement of Old Things** — *worn or out of date*
3. **Compulsory** — *forced by external factors*
4. **Fear** — *prevent or avoid disaster*

WANT — Look and Feel Better

5. **Esteem related** — *prestige or aspirational*
6. **Fad / Innovation** — *want the latest and greatest*
7. **Indulgence** — *"you're worth it"*
8. **Affiliation Identity** — *helps you connect*

If you're in the business of helping people look and/or feel better, you need to know when your customers want your product. For example, nail polish is not a necessity of life for any of us. People have lived for centuries without colored finger- and toenails, yet today, this is a multi-billion-dollar industry that meets the needs of women and men who want to look and feel better. When my wife gets her nails professionally done, she feels better about how she looks. Unfortunately, because we are small business owners who have to watch every dollar, getting her nails done at her favorite nail salon is an indulgence.

WANT VS. NEED

When the driving motivation for a purchase is a want, rather than a need, you have to be even savvier in your product development. Consider Premium Nails, one of our Design Dynamics POP Display customers. They are an acrylic nail polish manufacturer targeting the nail professionals, who serve people driven by want more than need.

Premium Nails knows that nail professionals lose time when they have to wait for the acrylic resin to cure before they can move onto the next nail. Time means money. It was a wise move offering a product that has a medium set-time for easy application. It also offered medium cure-time. This allows the nail professional to apply several nails in sequence, before pressing in the "C-Curve," a nail product they offer with a stronger, more-durable bond. That is a win-win for the customer and the salon professional.

Why do these product performance attributes matter? Nail professionals make more money when applying artificial nails working with a product that provides 100% retention onto natural nails, and leaves a smooth satin finish. This provides a service where there is little filing required, and a minimal release of airborne dust. By buying and using products that provide secure adhesion to natural nails, nail professionals can save time while insuring healthy natural nails for their client.

SOLVE A PROBLEM, FILL A NEED

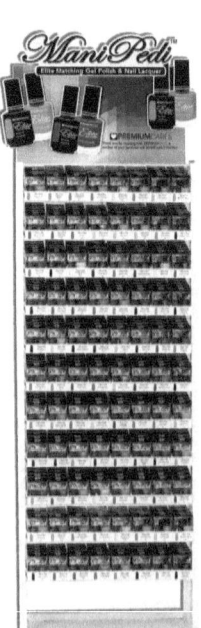

Because acrylic polish from Premium Nails is so easy to apply, the nail professional now controls the application, rather than having to wait for the product to set up. The acrylic resin made by Premium Nails has positively impacted the ManiPedi industry. They are at the forefront of providing the most beautiful, natural-looking product on the market today, in all colors, to enhance and complement all skin tones.

They're creating "the look that today's woman is searching for." This tagline from Premium Nails is key to appreciating the difference between serving a need and satisfying a want. You'll find that most potential customers have been searching for exactly what they want, and when they find it, they know it. These people are very likely to become the most valuable of customers: a repeat customer. Repeat customers are the backbone of almost all successful "great" business, like yours and mine.

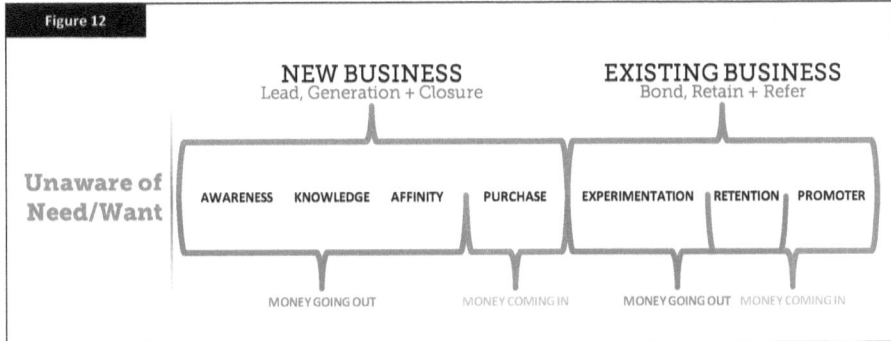
Figure 12

Too often, business leaders believe that consumers go from initial awareness, straight to purchase. But this rarely happens, and when it does, the odds of the customer being satisfied with their impulse purchase are typically quite low. The more clearly you understand the when behind a customer's purchase decision, the less likely you are to skip over these important stages: awareness, knowledge, and product affinity. All of these must occur before a customer's purchase decision is made. This reality can be seen through the above "consumer to retained customer" progression model:

Ideally, marketing and sales investments should be designed to help potential customers build knowledge of, and affinity for, the products and services your business offers. People won't purchase with confidence until they know how your product will benefit them. They won't purchase with enthusiasm until they develop an affinity for, or an attraction to, your product.

SPIN SELLING

In the book **SPIN Selling,** by Neil Rackham, SPIN stands for Situation – Problem – Implication – Need Payoff. According to Mr. Rackham, spur-of-the moment decisions are often irrational, and they're much more common in small sales than in large.

As the purchase price becomes larger, the following factors come into play:

- **Needs take longer to develop.**
- **Needs are likely to involve elements, influences and inputs from several people, and are not simply the wishes of a single individual.**
- **Needs are more likely to be expressed on a rational basis; even if the customer's underlying motivation is emotional or irrational, the need will usually require a rational justification.**
- **A purchasing decision that does not adequately meet the need is likely to have a more serious consequence for the decision maker.**

Think back on any major purchase you have made: As you became aware of the need or developed the want for the product, you began to identify where you could buy it. Depending on the importance of the need to be served or the want to be satisfied, you began to search out where to make your purchase.

EXPENSIVE-EAGER

The more important the item, the more effort you were willing to put forth. It's a process, and as you build your knowledge about the product and its potential benefits you will either see the benefits of owning or you won't.

If you develop affinity for the product you are considering, you are more likely to make the purchase. If you fail to develop affinity for the product, the only time you make the purchase is when you are being forced to by some outside influence.

Consider the proof of insurance mandate in the Affordable Healthcare Act. This mandate upsets a lot of people who are forced to buy insurance or face a tax penalty for not having it. The problem is that those who are being forced to buy health insurance are becoming increasingly vocal regarding what they don't like about the product. When compelled to buy, it is rarely a satisfying purchase.

In *SPIN Selling*, Rackham defined a need as: "any statement made by the buyer which expresses a want or concern that can be satisfied by the seller." He goes onto say that the first sign of a need is a slight discontent or dissatisfaction—one that is likely to grow. There is a final step in the development of a need: the "problem to be solved" is translated into "a want, a desire, or an intention to act." Needs normally start with minor imperfections, but will eventually evolve into clear problems, difficulties, or dissatisfactions, before finally becoming wants, desires, or intentions to act. It's a progression.

COST:BENEFIT RATIO

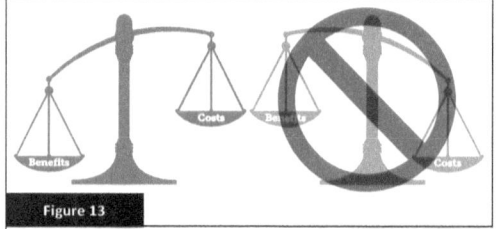
Figure 13

The affinity necessary to act on our knowledge is relative to the size of the need and the cost of a solution. It's the old cost: benefit ratio. If the customer perceives the problem to be larger than the cost of solving it, then there will probably be a purchase. If the problem is small and the cost high, the sale is unlikely.

DON'T SKIP THE AFFINITY STEP

When I joined VPI as an elected officer and senior executive, I was assigned by the Board of Directors to lead the development of a fact-based, segmented and targeted approach to improving revenue generation. I was accountable for a sixteen million dollar operating budget and a team of eighty marketing, communications and sales people.

The key to my success was in creating quality leads that could be converted and retained through the establishment of a defined marketing management process; this then became the catalyst for defining and executing our new and improved business strategy. Before I assumed responsibility for marketing, VPI followed no structured approach. Through the application of strategy, structure and process, I was able to efficiently and effectively identify critical success factors, and then translate them into clear objectives and practical action plans. I used the "consumer to retained customer" progression model to focus our organizational efforts on making changes that added the most value, by creating organizational alignment, setting priorities and allocating resources to strategic priorities.

On the sales front, our problem was clear: we'd been skipping over the affinity step through our sales conversation. People would call in wanting to learn about pet health insurance. Our sales agents would answer their questions, giving the prospective customer some knowledge about the product, and then quickly move them on to making a purchase decision, as fast as they could. They were very focused on getting to the next caller, because they were being paid 100% on commission.

...our new strategy needed to focus on building an affinity with them...

This strategy worked for the few impulse buyers we get each day, but not for those who really wanted to understand how our pet health insurance would help them provide better healthcare for their pets. These thoughtful "pet parents" were our "best customers," and our new strategy needed to focus on building an affinity with them.

Skipping the affinity step also killed our policyholder retention rates. Any time you buy a product for the very first time, you immediately move into an "experimentation mode," where you focus on either validating the wisdom of your purchase decision, or questioning your sanity. When your affinity for the product is grounded in true knowledge of how the product will benefit you, validation is often the result. But when your purchase is more impulse driven, your experience may not be what you expected, and you are at risk of becoming dissatisfied with the purchase. If you are really dissatisfied, you're likely to either return the product or share your dissatisfaction with others. Either way, you won't become a retained customer, a repeat customer, or one who has good things to say to others about your consumer experience.

RETAIN THE CUSTOMER

I employed the "consumer to retained customer" progression model (Figure 12) at VPI to re-focus the sales department onto our new needs-based sales model. In making this key change I replaced the top-down sales model, which had been employed for over twenty years. This major initiative resulted in forty million dollars of direct annual phone sales, while also improving sales agent morale, productivity and retention. By implementing these sales conversion improvements, such as shifting to a needs-based approach, our phone conversion rate reached 36%, even after increasing our product price by 20%.

Becoming more thoughtful at VPI, in how we guided people through the purchase decision process, produced dramatic results. We increased policyholder retention from 72% to 77%, gross revenues from $128M to $197M and profits grew to reach $8.2M, all within three years. This was accomplished through the generation of over 1.1 billion impressions that led to more than 1.2 million leads, resulting in 17% revenue growth, even during the deep recession of 2008.

MARKETING AND SALES

To own a great business, you need to continuously invest in marketing and sales. How will your sales improve if you aren't efficiently and creatively promoting yourself? The never-ending challenge is in knowing which promotions are worth the money, and which are not. For more on how to recognize and make better promotional decisions, see Chapter 8 beginning on page 81.

The success of any television show is directly related to recognizing the best night and time slot in which to air the show. For example, by the end of 1994–95, Murder She Wrote's eleventh season, Angela Lansbury was content to continue with the series. However, her advancing age, as she turned seventy, had become a concern to the producers and the network. As a result, CBS made the decision to move the show to Thursday nights at 8 p.m. This change was made after Murder She Wrote had aired for nearly eleven years on Sunday nights. But this put the series in direct competition with the first hour of NBC's "Must See TV" comedy lineup, which had been drawing the highest ratings of the week for any network for years.

> *How will your sales improve if you aren't efficiently and creatively promoting yourself?*

Despite protests from the show's fans, who believed that CBS was intentionally setting the show up to fail in its new time-slot, CBS refused to budge. And in its twelfth season, Murder She Wrote plummeted from 8th to 58th in the yearly ratings, losing nearly six million viewers, as the audience failed to follow it to its new day and time. To soften the blow of canceling a much-loved show, the network agreed to air the final four episodes in the original Sunday night time-slot, as well as commission four Murder, She Wrote movies over the next few years. This provided the hit series and its loyal viewers with an acceptable send-off.

WHEN—RIGHT NOW

The when really matters to your businesses success. There is an absolute, direct correlation between when your customers are most likely to need your help, and when they are most likely to buy from you. It's amazing to me how focused

we can become when we want to make something happen. And the greater this sense of urgency, the higher the probability that we will buy.

The good news is that when customers approach you with any of these above post-it notes, literally or metaphorically, the question becomes who they will be buying from, because their when is already established. By asking the right questions and discovering the when related to the customer's need or want, you'll have identified the key to timing

The only thing that will keep you from realizing a sale in these situations is your inability to deliver the desired product or service.

and message-vehicle selection for your marketing and promotional investments. When you have a product that appeals to a broad customer base, when becomes a critical success factor. The only thing that will keep you from realizing a sale in these situations is your inability to deliver the desired product or service.

As Design Dynamics we compete on urgency, confusion and quality. We serve a broad market with numerous competitors offering similar, or in many cases, the identical visual communication products that we create. What helps us win in the marketplace is our depth of talent and breadth of capabilities. We do particularly well when people need same-day or next-day delivery. This ability to turn jobs quickly helps us better serve our customers, which, in turn, keeps them coming back and prompts them to refer us to others.

What is your turn around time? What is your most critical success factor? You have one; perhaps you just need to reflect on what it is most customers ask for when they call you.

In a perfect world, the best time to promote to your target customer is just before they need your solution. (Selling snow tires in November works better than in July, at least in the Northern hemisphere. Swimsuits? Not so much...) Unfortunately, we don't live in a perfect world. This means that you need to clearly and precisely identify when people will need or want the products and services your business can provide. It's one of the best ways you can help your customers buy the things they need, while helping your business succeed.

CHAPTER SIX
4th ORGANIZING PRINCIPLE: WHERE?
Place: Part Two

Two of the seven organizing principles are associated with "place." You start with when your target customer will want to purchase your solution. Knowing when focuses your promotion and sales timing so that the fourth principle, where positions you at the place your customer will want to purchase from you.

PLACE AND LOCATION

"Place" involves two factors: the location of the market, and the means of distribution in reaching it. Simply put, place is where you and your customer transact the sale. Your marketing challenge is to generate continuous traffic to the place your target chooses to transact business, not where you want to do it.

If you serve a well-defined geographic market, then the three keys to your success are location, location, and location. Anytime the three L's are associated with your business, where will be your number one organizing principle, on which to build your business success.

On the other hand, if 100% of your customers purchase online from you, then your focus is on driving traffic to your website. In this case, the where is the online marketplace. Customers have a lot of choices these days about how, and where, to make their purchases. Ignore their preferences, and you won't be in business for long.

> **Customers have a lot of choices these days about how, and where, to make their purchases. Ignore their preferences, and you won't be in business for long.**

DON'T LOSE OUT ON A SALE

You'll lose a sale if you aren't where your customer wants to purchase the product, and you'll lose a sale if you fail to offer the type of relationship your customers prefers.

I'll give you just a quick example. An outdoor equipment company specializing in the resale of used but serviceable equipment has a small retail storefront. Their target customer is a college student with limited income and a desire to purchase good quality used equipment for the lowest price. Their customers do a lot of comparison-shopping in order to reach this goal, cruising online vendors offering "seconds," as well as craigslist and eBay.

They've very Internet savvy folks. Yet this particular outdoor equipment company has no website, and no online inventory of the goods they're offering for sale. Customers cannot purchase from this outdoor equipment company online. They can't even check out what's for sale! And so, unless the customer happens to walk in their store, they're going to lose out on a lot of sales. In this day and age, it seems a foolish way to operate any business.

The process of learning where your customers want to purchase from you begins as you develop your who, what, and when insights. You began by learning who is most likely to benefit from what you do, and this was followed by learning exactly when the customer is most likely to purchase what you have to offer. To find clarity on where your customers want to complete their transactions, it's important to ask yourself this simple question: do they know where to find you?

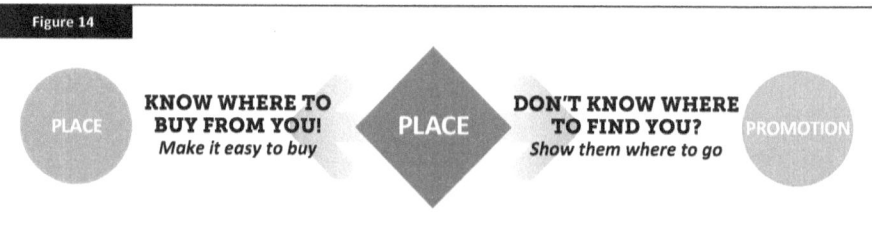

Figure 14

WHERE ARE YOU

When people don't know where to find you, your marketing is all about promotion. Your goal is to show them where to go to buy what they need. Once they know where to buy from you, it's all about making it easy for them to buy from you. When your customers know where to buy, you no longer have to invest any promotional resources on "place."

Place matters because it's where the exchange of value takes place, where your business delivers the service, or satisfies the want or need, to your customer, at a profit to you. If you don't provide people with an easy and convenient location in which to purchase from you, you'll lose out on sales nearly 100% of the time to any of your competitors who do.

THE POWER OF PLACE

To appreciate the power of place in driving improved business results, consider Hostess Brands, the iconic maker of snack cakes including Twinkies, Ho Hos, Ding Dongs and Donettes. In 2013, following the bankruptcy protection proceedings of the original company, the newly reorganized company emerged from a painful corporate restructuring. And it was doing better than expected, due to a series of smart moves by the new management team, under the ownership of private investors Apollo Global and C. Dean Metropoulos.

When the Standard and Poor's (S&P) upgraded its "recovery rating" on the Hostess Brands company to "2," indicating that even if the company were to default, lenders could expect to get upwards of 90% of their investment back.

The company said, they are focused on growing their sales base through new products and continued expansion into channels where they historically had not maintained a significant presence, such as dollar stores and vending. They were letting their customers know where to find the products they had grown to love. Smart move. Could you do this with your product or company?

Since the re-launch of the business in July 2013, the company has re-established its brands and regained good market share, S&P's report stated. New channels = new business. And it worked.

IN CONTRAST

There are many stories describing the shortsightedness of companies when it comes to location. Way back when railroads were the up-and-coming mode of transportation, waterways were still the leading mode of transportation for commerce. As the country pushed West and cattle became a big commodity, train companies approached Cincinnati with a proposal to build a massive stockyard in that location. They knew Cincinnati was a leading point of commerce on the Ohio River, and was also near the Mississippi River. But Cincinnati turned them down, saying, "Trains will never replace water transport." Cincinnati's city leaders felt secure in the status quo, and so the train companies approached another city—Chicago.

> *When you know where your customers prefer to buy, you're better positioned to drive the right traffic to your business...*

Other factors also contributed to the success of Chicago in becoming a leading rail center, including the Mississippi River's blockade by Union and Confederate armies during the civil war. Yet in the end, the windy city became the second largest city in the U.S. until 1990 and it continues now to be the third largest city in the country.

When you know where your customers prefer to buy, you're better positioned to drive the right traffic to your business, the group of customers you can most easily convert and retain. Driving the "right" traffic is tied to the customer's transaction preference. You won't complete profitable sales transactions unless you are where your customer wants to transact business, and you're able to do so in the way your customer most desires.

Figure 15

PHYSICAL LOCATION
People Skills + Environment

PLACE

ONLINE
Web + Social Media Presence

If your business is dependent on a physical location, the in-store experience you offer must be better than their online experience, or they won't come back. This means you need to engage employees who will provide your customers with a service experience they can't get online, and maintain a product inventory, so they'll leave your store with a great experience, and the product they came for in hand.

GOOGLE THE ADDRESS

Prior to the web, customers depended on the Yellow Pages to locate small businesses. Now customers will find your business through Internet searches where SEO (search engine optimization) or PPC (pay per clicks) are going to be the driving forces. SEO refers to the process of improving traffic to your website by increasing your site's visibility in search engine results.

> *...you need to engage employees who will provide your customers with a service experience they can't get online...*

You improve your website's SEO by continuously investing in your content, making sure that your pages can be indexed correctly, and that your content is unique and genuine. When you do this, you are more likely to increase traffic to your site because the site will appear higher in search results for information that pertains to your site's offerings. Junk sites with poor content will not rank as well.

ARE YOU ONLINE

SEO is tough, yet is key if you are reliant on the Internet for your business. If the Internet is where you primarily conduct business, then you are likely to also be investing in pay-per-clicks (PPC) to drive traffic to your site. PPC is an advertising model, implemented by search engines like Google and Yahoo, as well as other websites, that charges businesses for advertising each time a site visitor clicks on your specific link. When the site visitor clicks on your link, the click is registered in a system and a pre-determined charge is assessed. One of the most popular pay-per-clicks programs is Google's Ad Words.

At VPI, we spent a lot of money on PPC, yet I've never thought it was the most effective form of advertising for us. It was definitely better than print magazine advertising, yet it was never as effective as a quality article on the value of pet insurance, placed in a trusted publication.

INTERNET MARKETING

At Design Dynamics, I do everything I can to improve our SEO performance, but I won't touch PPC. Why? Because I want people to connect with us because they see value in our site and believe that we can help them—not because they clicked on an ad they think will get them a bargain price on their banner. We aren't in the business of selling cheap banners; we are leaving this market for others to serve.

Figure 16

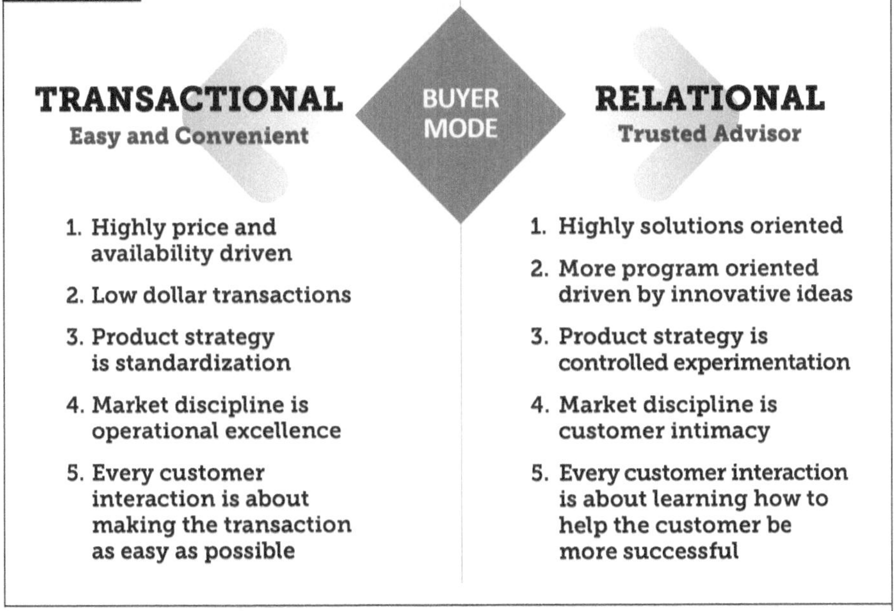

TRANSACTIONAL
Easy and Convenient

BUYER MODE

RELATIONAL
Trusted Advisor

1. Highly price and availability driven
2. Low dollar transactions
3. Product strategy is standardization
4. Market discipline is operational excellence
5. Every customer interaction is about making the transaction as easy as possible

1. Highly solutions oriented
2. More program oriented driven by innovative ideas
3. Product strategy is controlled experimentation
4. Market discipline is customer intimacy
5. Every customer interaction is about learning how to help the customer be more successful

Wherever the transaction preference exists, the expectations of your customer are proportionate to the money they spend with you. This is why it's important to understand the type of relationship your target customer desires to have with you, as the second part of answering the where question.

The buying mode your customer uses to approach a transaction will determine the type of relationship they want to have with you. The more their buyer mode tilts toward relational, the greater the degree of service your target will expect as part of their business transaction.

As you think about the type of relationship your customer wants to have with you, and you with them, the next question to answer is whether your target customer is willing to pay for the level of service they expect, or, is it all about obtaining the lowest possible price? What's really driving their purchase decision?

At Design Dynamics, we've identified three tiers of customers (see Table 1 on the next page): Tier 1 customers are tough for us. We aren't the lowest cost producer; instead, we focus on quality, so we provide good value, and as a result we're better structured to serve Tier 2 and Tier 3 customers. People who need a graphics and signage expert to guide them to the best solution are more appropriate customers for us than those who already know exactly what they want. I believe in the saying, "you can't be all things to all people," so, at Design Dynamics, we chose to matter to those who value our depth of experience and breadth of capability.

TABLE 1

Tier One	Tier Two	Tier Three
They know exactly what they want and they don't care where they get it	They need "Expert" validation and/or advice to validate w-hat they think they need	They want the help of the "authority" so they get the best results
Prefer to buy online	Prefer email, telephone is OK	Want to initiate through in-person interaction
Price is the #1 motivator	Quality & service is important at a good value	Want to innovate, looking for custom solutions
No help needed	Some help needed from someone they trust	Confused about the best solution and need someone they trust and like to guide them
Willing to wait for ground shipping from a cheaper source	Planned so time exists to buy smart yet prefer to buy locally from someone they know and trust	Urgent need because someone failed to plan that needs same or next day delivery
Expect a discount or they won't give you the order	Willing to pay our price if seen as a good value	Less concerned about price, more concerned about getting what they want when they want it
No loyalty, will shop around every time	Will subject us to competitive bids to ensure they get a good value	Will only buy from us with no competitive bids
OK	**Good**	**Evangelist**

I have also found this framework helpful relative to thinking through the implications associated with "when" and "where" for my business. If the answer to "when" is today, then they aren't likely to get the product they want online. If they have time on their side because they planned ahead for their need and are willing to shop, you are going to be in a price-competitive situation.

If they have time, you have options for producing the desired quality. If they need quality now, then it's going to cost them a premium...

If they want quality, the question becomes one of time: If they have time, you have options for producing the desired quality. If they need quality now, then it's going to cost them a premium, because it is going to cost you more to produce the product quickly, particularly if you have to hijack your production processes to produce their order outside of your typical lead-times.

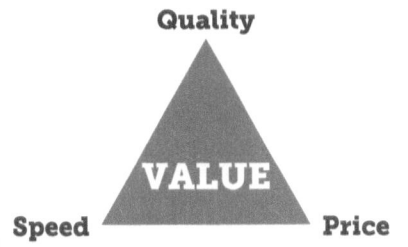

Figure 17

GOOD, CHEAP SERVICE won't be **FAST**
FAST, CHEAP SERVICE won't be **GOOD**
GOOD, FAST SERVICE won't be **CHEAP**
GOOD, FAST & CHEAP is **UNLIKELY**

VALUE TRIANGLE

Another way to think about your business's preferred customer type is to look at the "value triangle" of quality, speed and price, reflected in Figure 17. It's commonly understood that you can have any two of these values, but not all three. Because this simple statement is a truism, it provides an excellent framework for considering the price sensitivity attributes of your customers. For example, if you live in Los Angeles and you just learned that you need to be in New York City tomorrow morning, it's going to cost you a high premium to get there. Your need to be there quickly robs you of the alternative to fly more economically. Whereas, if you know in advance of your need to be in New York City, then you have time to shop for the best airfare.

Great businesses are built around the need to provide a product or service quickly. They have the infrastructure in place to turn things around fast. The downside is that this ability is associated with higher costs—so services like this won't be a bargain for the customer. Think FedEx. Then think about the local courier service who will deliver your package even faster than FedEx. Your delivery is the only one they care about when you transact with them. The good news is that you know it will get there when you need it to; the bad news is that it's going to cost more money for this speed and convenience.

"Great businesses are built around the need to provide a product or service quickly."

Great businesses are also built around providing good products at the lowest prices. The challenge with these highly process-disciplined businesses is they can't deal with rush orders; if what you are seeking is not on their shelf ready to hand over to you, then it's going to take as long as it's going to take. Vistaprint is a great example of this. You can go to vistaprint.com right now and order 500 business cards for $20, if you are prepared to upload your own art and wait for them to print and ship your cards. This actually works great in most cases, but not if you need your cards for an event you are attending this evening. If this were the case, I would send you to Whitener Graphics. They'll produce your cards for you while you wait.

TABLE 2			
	Good	**Better**	**Best**
Quality	Meets "Just Enough"	Meets All Requirements	Exceeds Requirements
Speed (time)	7 Business Days	3 Business Days	Next Business Day
Service (touch)	No Touch Self Service Online	Some Touch Phone and eMail Order Confirmation	Face-to-Face Consulting
Price	**Bargain** Sacrifice S & Q to get cheapest Price	**Good Value** Pay a little more for good S & Q	**Premium** Pay above average for premium S & Q

For my own business, I like to look at the value triangle from the perspective of good, better and best. I also look at production speed from a time and "touch," or service, perspective as in the following:

When you know where your customer wants to purchase from you, as well as what type of relationship they want to have with you, then you can structure your core processes to deliver in a way that is highly valued by your customer. "Valued by your customer" means that they are willing to pay a price that allows you to make a fair return on your materials, labor and overhead.

Before you look at Table 3, the "Process Step" table for Design Dynamics, on the next page, it's important to understand the green circle, blue square, and black diamond column labeling, which come straight from the ski slopes.

I love to snowboard with my son, and ski with my daughter. One of the universally accepted guides to ski resort trail maps is the use of green circles to indicate beginner runs, identifying the easiest way down the mountain. Blue squares are for intermediate runs, and black diamonds are for advanced skiers only. I use this same logic to differentiate the "degree of difficulty" associated with how we execute a production process to meet a particular customer need.

TABLE 3

Process Step	Green Circle	Blue Square	⬛ Black Diamond
Sales and Service	No Touch No customer interaction	Some Touch Serviced mostly by phone and email	High Touch In person service
Quote	Standard Pricing List price	Standard Product with Known Materials and Processes Standard pricing	Never Been Done Before or Custom with Multiple Variables Added services get their own line item on quotes and invoices
Design	Self Service Online	Basic Layout Large format print Quality confirmation	Concept, Design, Production and Finishing
Prepress	None	High Quality Customer Supplied Art 1-5 versions Same material	Customer Supplied Art Must Be Enhanced More than 5 Versions More than 3 sizes Custom color match
Material	Scrap	In-stock or at Distributor for Next Day Delivery	Custom Order, One Project Use
Print	Gang Run with Similar Jobs	Standard Material Setup and Printing With a minimum three days to finish	Stop Schedule Workflow for special set-up
Finish Lamination	No Lamination	Polyester or Calendar Matte Overlam	UV Cast Overlam
Finish-Cutting	No Machine Cutting	Keen Cut Summa, Die, or Guillotine	Router Hand Cut
Finish Composition	None	Weed Hem and Grommet	App Tape Sewn
Package	None	Paper, Plastic or Stock Cardboard	Custom Made Box
Deliver	Customer Pickup	UPS	In-Person By Design Dynamics
Install	Single Person No special equipment	2+ People Local equipment rental and parts purchase	Specialized / Hire Out
Invoice	Pay on Delivery	30-Day Terms	50% Deposit Required

DEGREE OF DIFFICULTY

As you see in our core process Table 3, we have to work through a number of processes to meet the needs of our Tier-2 and Tier-3 customers. Within each process, there are a number of different approaches we can take. By knowing their buyer mode and which element of the value triangle is most important to them, we are better able to adapt our process to produce the best result for our customer, at a price they are willing to pay that has profit within it for us.

> *...your employees—they're literally the "face" of your business...*

I discuss process in the chapter on where, because your customer ultimately experiences the majority of your processes where the exchange of value occurs. Your place of business is also where your customers are going to encounter your employees—they're literally the "face" of your business, and this is important.

If you're investing a lot of money to be in a particular location, and you've done everything you can to create an inviting environment to do business in, you may still lose a sale if your employees aren't on board with the experience you are trying to provide for your customer. If this is the case, you'd be better off dumping the physical location and doing business entirely online. It's essential to ensure that your employees deliver the customer experience you know is required to win over your target customer.

BACK TO CRIME SHOWS

The where is of great importance in any crime drama. The crime must take place in proximity to our main characters, in order for the story to be told, and for the audience to tune in.

Often, the murder takes place in the jurisdiction of the main character's precinct or division. However, in Murder She Wrote (CBS, 1984-1996), any locale visited by Angela Lansbury as "Jessica Fletcher" was immediately stalked by death moments after her arrival. Wherever mystery author Jessica Fletcher was, a murder would occur nearby, and the show's writers brilliantly made this believable.

This genius by the show's producers, Richard Levinson, William Link and writer-producer Peter S. Fischer, was confirmed by producing 264 episodes over 12 seasons, in which their main character, Jessica Fletcher, solved different murders while allowing us to join in her travels as a famed mystery writer.

If the where for Murder, She Wrote had been solely based on her primary residence in Cabot Cove, a cozy coastal town in Maine, the show would have soon run out of storylines to intrigue us. As we tagged along with Jessica on her book tours and visits to family and friends, we saw her show greater perception than the official investigators, who were always a little too quick to arrest the most likely suspect.

It was Jessica's astute piecing together of the clues through her "who, what, when, where, how, and especially why questions that allowed her to trap the real murderer, in every episode.

"There are always door openings. And gradually, it accumulates. The opportunities open up in front of you."

BUZZ ALDRIN

CHAPTER SEVEN

5th ORGANIZING PRINCIPLE: WHY?
People

If you've ever spent time with a young child, you will likely have heard the question, "Why?" Asking the question, "why?" is natural to children, because they want to understand what's happening in their environment, and they have an insatiable desire to learn. In essence, they're engaged in gathering information. And so are your customers.

This is an excellent character trait for all entrepreneurs: to continue asking why? And why not? And why not me? A successful and great business is based on problem solving and there is always a why behind a problem.

The answer to why has to be clear, in every message you send both spoken and written and in every decision you make. It's really why that runs parallel to every question you ask and every answer you provide, to the "who, what, when, where, and how" of running a great business.

For example:

- Who is your target customer, and why?
- What problem is your customer trying to solve, and why?
- When is your customer most likely to need your help, and why?
- Where will your customer want to transact business, and why?
- How should your customer value what you do at a price that allows you to earn a profit, and why?

When you incorporate why in these fundamental information-organizing questions, you increase the "degree of difficulty" associated with creating an actionable answer on which to stake your business decisions.

WHY ASK WHY

For your success in business, defining the why starts with leadership. It is held together by your culture, anchored by your strategic style, and embodied by your employees.

Not knowing the why behind what they're offering to the customer creates disconnects between your employees and your business's leadership.

Throughout my career, it's never ceased to amaze me when employees fail to make the connection between the importance of money coming into a business through a customer purchase and the money going out to them in their paycheck.

They seem to feel little ownership or responsibility, and they do not see that the monies paid to them each payday flow directly from the monies paid by the customer for the goods and services they purchase. This disconnect can show up as poor customer service, which in turn affects the customer's ability to see value in what you are selling, and in their own experience. If they fail to see and experience this value, you are not likely to experience a profit on that sale.

> *The most successful businesses help the employees feel a sense of ownership, not only in the company, but also in the culture.*

The most successful businesses help the employees feel a sense of ownership, not only in the company, but also in the culture. I have a sign on my desk that says "It is better to have one person work with you than three people work for you."

You solve the question of why by clearly understanding your customer value proposition, and stating it, so that your employees can also understand how they create value for your customer in the work that they do.

This is a very important point that I hope you'll read twice. Once you know who your customer is, what problem they are trying to solve, when they are most likely to need your help, and where they will want to transact business, you can confidently define why they should value what you do. This forms the reason to believe in what you do, for both your customers and your employees.

CHOOSING YOUR STRATEGIC STYLE

In the book *Discipline of Market Leaders,* authors Michael Treacy and Fred Wiersema describe a process in which customers search for operational excellence, product leadership, and customer intimacy as three sources of value. Their premise is that the source of value you choose to build from defines your company's strategic style.

Figure 18

CLARITY OR CONFUSION

When the leaders of a company fail to create clarity on the strategic style for their business, customers become confused. It is particularly baffling to customers when their expectations are not matched, or when the company's employees don't know how to deliver the expected value.

This is because the strategic style you follow shapes your business culture and the behaviors of everyone associated with your company, from your employees to your customers. No company in the world is a leader in all three disciplines: operational excellence, product leadership and customer intimacy. Your goal is to be world-class in your chosen discipline, and very competitive in the other two disciplines.

COME FLY WITH ME

Do you approach flying with Southwest differently than you do United or Delta? This is because the strategic style chosen by Southwest Airlines has shaped the way you approach them. Boarding a Southwest flight is driven by your boarding position, which, in turn, is driven by your group assignment. So, you try to check-in to your flight with Southwest as soon as you can (no earlier than 24 hours prior to your flight), so that you can get into group A. You can live with group B, but group C puts you at risk of ending up with a middle seat.

Southwest Airlines knows that people don't like being in groups B or C, so they've found a way to monetize your dislike by charging you additional money for priority boarding, through their Business Select® fare. If you are like me and don't want to pay for this "guarantee," then your strategy is all about timing your check-in earlier than everyone else on your flight. The faster you check-in online, the earlier your assigned spot will come up when your group is released to board the plane. I hate this process, and this is why Southwest is my last choice to fly if I have a choice of carriers to my desired destination. So does this strategy work with their customers? Not me.

The strategic style you choose to do business with defines the why for everyone associated with your company. It's best determined by how you define the who, what, when and where for your business. You simply can't do it all, nor can you be all things to all people, so you must play to your strengths by doing what your business is naturally best at.

Precise clarity on the why gives you the ability to teach your employees why what they do matters to the customer. The hard reality is that if your employees aren't clear on the why behind what they do, they will waste resources and jeopardize your ability to cost-effectively produce your products. This is a particular killer if your strategic style is operational excellence and you are competing strongly on price.

If your customer service doesn't meet expectations, your customers won't keep coming back with repeat business, nor will they refer you to others. This is a sure way to go out of business, particularly if you are competing strongly on customer intimacy.

Determine your strategic style, then use it to anchor your customer value proposition, while helping your employees understand how to perform with excellence and demonstrate a high level of quality service. Employees want to be part of a winning team; they are looking to you for leadership and guidance.

Great businesses have great teams who enjoy the people they work with, trust the people they work for and believe in the product they are selling.

GREAT PLACE TO WORK

In the book *The Talent Solution,* Edward L. Gubman provides some excellent thinking on aligning strategy and people to achieve extraordinary results. Gubman illustrates the process by which companies with strong cultures choose people who are the right "fit". When you select employees who "fit" with your values, you'll go a long way to ensuring value alignment and a strong company culture. New employees will be brought into your organization predisposed to hear what you have to say and prepared to buy into what you are trying to accomplish.

> **When you select employees who "fit" with your values, you'll go a long way to ensuring value alignment and a strong company culture...**

Suspicion and cynicism will be reduced because you will be hiring someone who is a closer match for the business culture your style of leadership shaped. I very much appreciated Gubman's Strategic Styles Framework (Table 4 is adapted from *The Talent Solution*, on the next page).

Hire people who closely fit your strategic style and teach them to competently perform their duties. It's unrealistic to expect flawless execution from your employees, particularly if they're unable to see the "value creation" in what they do. No plan completely survives the battlefield.

The mark of a great business owner is not constant, flawless execution; it's how well you, and those who work for you, respond to the problems that arise. An employee's ability to respond to customer issues is proportionate to how well they understand your unique value proposition, and their own role in the process.

The highest praise you can give an employee is to call them a "problem solver." Empower them to solve the "little problems" so there won't be as many "big problems" on your plate.

TABLE 4

	Operations *Operational Excellence*	**Products** *Product Leadership*	**Customers** *Customer Intimacy*
Founding Concept	Deliver low-cost, reliable & easy-to-use products and services	Deliver Leading Edge Products	Provide Highly Customized Solutions and Services
Examples	Cargill, Southwest Airlines, Lincoln Electric, Target Stores, Whirlpool	W.L. Gore, Nike, 3M, Motorola, Bloomingdales	IBM, Nordstrom, Johnson Controls, USAA
Most Critical Business Need	Standardization is key to efficiency	Creative process has to come first	Creation of customized solutions that produce distinctive results for customers
Source of Alignment	Goals and Results	Technical activities & resources	Values
Core Capability	Consistent application	Constant innovation	In-depth relationship building
Management Style	Manage top-down	Manage inside-out	Manage outside-in, or bottom-up
Leadership Type	Charismatic; likes to make things happen	Quiet thinker; takes time to pursue the big picture and encourages others to do it, too	Strong appeals to values; concerned about how people feel and wants them to enjoy their jobs, careers, organizations, and, ultimately, lives
Natural Inclinations/ Interests of Employees	Making things	Ideas	People
Lead Talent Management Practice	Performance-based compensation	Fluid organization	Selection for fit
Employee	Process control	Life-long learning	Relationship building
Competencies	Continuous improvement, teamwork, analysis, financial/operational understanding, group facilitation, attention to detail, drive for results	Information sharing, curiosity, creativity, group problem-solving, breakthrough thinking, artistic, visionary	Listening, rapid problem-solving, independent action initiative, collaboration, quality-focused, understand motivation
Expectations of Employees	Employees deliver standardized products and services with great cost/value relationships for customers	Employees are enable to create leading-edge products	Employees provide customized solutions to meet unique customer needs or terrific service that goes well beyond competitive offerings
Work Environment	Stable, predictable, measurable, hierarchical, cost conscious, team-based, formal, compliant, "If it ain't broke, Break it bit-by-bit"	Exciting, experimental, learning-focused, technical, informal, fast-paced, resource-rich, comfortable, constantly changing, speed-to-market, "If we build it, they will come"	Values driven, dynamic, changing, informal, collegial, conversational, few policies, service oriented, qualitative, bottoms-up, employee as customer, "Whatever it takes"
Workforce Strategy	Efficiency, order, and process are the foundation for building teams to deliver high-value, low-cost processes with heavy emphasis on everyone knowing the rules and playing by them	Provide a comfortable, resource-rich environment that allows people to be creative	Responsiveness, selection, socialization, and autonomy are the core employee issues that make it easier for front-line employees to serve customers with individualized help

LANDMINES OR LESSONS LEARNED

There are landmines everywhere in business. The hard reality is that, more often than not, there are things you can't completely control. This is why how you respond to situations that don't go as planned is so important. One of the benefits of the 7-P Framework is that it can help you work through the unseen landmines that can torpedo your business. This formula and method of thinking can be helping you make the best decisions you possibly can, in the moment.

The result of an overabundance of frustrated and stressed-out employees is strained resources. They'll be strained because the people who work with and for you are consumed in dealing with "unexpected" problems, not understanding that such problems are an ongoing and natural part of doing business. This response is aggravated when it is unclear exactly why people buy your products or utilize your services. And this customer value proposition needs to be clear, foundational information to all those who are expected to deliver your products and services. It can never be overlooked.

> *The result of an overabundance of frustrated and stressed-out employees is strained resources.*

LEADERSHIP IN GREAT BUSINESSES

Successful businesses have strong leaders and a culture that reinforces their values. They develop their strategic style and then use it to anchor their customer value proposition, while helping their employees learn the duties they are to perform. It's critical to know which of your employees is capable of making an independent judgment call in an unknown situation, one that closely models your own judgment. Then it's up to you to empower these individuals, who will, in turn, empower your organization to greater profitability. No man, or woman, is an island: If you have to be personally involved in every decision, you will likely fail.

In confirming the logic of the 7-P Framework for owning a great business, I reached out to my own business network's leaders to gather additional wisdom on why some businesses fail, and why others don't. I took these responses, mapped them, and traced them back to my 7-P Framework. Below is one of my favorite responses, which comes from Jack Parsons, an Ohio friend who has worked for the Honda Motor Company for nearly thirty years:

"It starts with the philosophy and culture of the organization. Organizations that are successful start with a noble purpose (something beyond making money). The leaders actually lead and align the people in the organization to deliver quality products and services to their customers, on time, and at a reasonable price. Processes and results are always visible and transparent. Gaps are quickly seen and marked as addressed".

INTENT

Jack continued, "Scientific problem-solving is employed, but it is not complex. It's about the '5 whys' and not the '5 whos.' Everyone is able to know if his/her job is helping the organization win on a daily basis. Everyone is doing today's job and also working on how to make the organization better, tomorrow. Leaders provide targets, and then guide and coach.

Work is standardized, but not so rigid as to restrict or impede change and improvement. Without a level of standardization, there can be no continuous improvement. It's important to look at not only what gets done, but also how it gets done. Many, repeated base hits are better than just a few home runs.

"Developing as many people in the organization for this type of learning will lead to success. Customers and suppliers are brought in to see internal processes and how everyone is linked in the value stream. Metrics are few and are more focused on the entire value stream and less on departmental silos. Customer-specific production groups linked with cross-functional support groups provide a laser-like focus, to provide the best products and services for their customers. People like coming to work. Customers can get what they want. They can have frank discussions with the provider, and the provider listens. These are some of my thoughts, off the top of my head."

What I appreciate about Jack's response is his wisdom relative to the importance of culture and leadership to a business's success. When you have strong leadership in place, no matter the size of your organization, you have the foundational building-blocks for success. If you also have a healthy culture that reinforces the values of your company, and a consistent pattern of response in handling problems that arise from interactions among employees, with customers, and within the business environment, you will also have the "mortar" that holds your disconnected building-blocks together. This leads to even greater success.

GREAT BUILDING BLOCKS ARE NOT A GUARANTEE TO SUCCESS

Another thoughtful response to my question on why businesses fail came from an executive I worked with at VPI. This excellent individual was recruited to be part of the leadership team at Nestle PurinaCare, a start-up pet health insurance competitor that had some of the best building blocks for success one could ever ask for. These building blocks began with a core leadership team of former VPI (the industry leader) pet health insurance executives who knew the industry well. Second, they had the financial backing of Nestle. (See the side bar on next page to appreciate just how significant the financial and marketing backing of Nestle was for PurinaCare.) Third, the team had designed a superior product, in comparison to what was currently being offered in the marketplace.

Industry	Food Processing
Founded	1866
Country	Switzerland
Employees	339,000
Sales	$100.08 B

RANKINGS ON FORBES LISTS:
#20 in Profits
#59 in Sales
#194 in Assets
#14 in Market Value
#43 Worlds Most Valuable Brands

Despite this promising beginning, Nestle pulled the plug on Nestle PurinaCare, on May 31, 2013, after more than five years of operation. But, to be fair, it's important to consider that Nestle's industry classification and expertise lie in food processing, not pet insurance. Just the same, Nestle did a lot of things right in launching their pet health insurance business, as evidenced by the following:

1. **The decision to enter the market place was made after a three-year study.**
2. **Three members of the PurinaCare executive team were experienced veterinarians.**
   a. They hired a CEO with an MBA, and a history as the former VP of customer-support for VPI.
   b. Their head of claims department was a retired Navy captain with a PhD in engineering.
   c. Their VP of operations was the former COO at VPI, who doubled as VP of Professional Relations.
3. **PurinaCare's pet insurance policy had the best premium value available— and it was easy to demonstrate and to sell.**
4. **It had an acceptable loss ratio on a downward trend.**
5. **Its policy was underwritten by a Berkshire Hathaway company.**
6. **PurinaCare's losses were underwritten by Nestle.**
7. **Its small team was located in a modest office in San Antonio.**
8. **The President of Nestle Purina, in St. Louis, was an enthusiastic believer and supporter.**

Well, that's quite a lot to build on. Those of us at VPI were very concerned about the launch of Nestle PurinaCare. Even with the solid, start-up, foundational building blocks in place, well suited to building a formidable pet health insurance company, they were ultimately unsuccessful.

You will see in the following analysis of "what went wrong," just how important culture and leadership are to avoiding business failure:

1. **Instead of relying on the experience and wisdom of his PurinaCare executive team, the Nestle Purina project head spent hundreds of thousands of dollars on consulting studies to justify his decisions;** while this is often typical for executives accustomed to working in a corporate environment, the money for those studies came out of the marketing budget.
2. **The PurinaCare executive team, made up of experienced individuals, was required to utilize the Nestle Purina in-house creative agency,** who unfortunately did not understand the pet health insurance business, and were very costly.
3. **Total money available for actual marketing was under $2 million.**
4. **There was a reasonable request to test the concept of hiring pet insurance reps for PurinaCare; this request was denied.** The reasoning was that the sixty or so Nestle Purina Professional Diet reps could take on the job. Unfortunately, that idea never got off the ground. The head of the pet diet division had his own sales numbers to worry about, and he wouldn't allow his reps to even discuss pet insurance.
5. **A major competitor initiated "legally-questionable" marketing strategies** (one-month free insurance to entice enrollments, paying his reps commissions, even though they were not licensed, etc.); Nestle Purina Legal would not address the situation in a way that would allow PurinaCare to compete.
6. **The President of Nestle Purina retired.** Soon after, his replacement expressed his lack of support for Nestle Purina to be in the pet health insurance business. Very quickly, his executive team fell in line with that thought.

    The example of PurinaCare shows the importance of leadership in establishing the "why" that runs parallel to every one of the answers to your who, what, where, when and how questions.

PurinaCare had excellent fundamentals in place, yet their corporate leadership was unclear on the value this new division was creating for their pet-loving customer base. As a result, they squandered an excellent opportunity to help highly bonded pet owners provide quality healthcare for their pets.

Such disconnects in any organization can have fatal consequences. I've come to strongly associate the fifth organizing principle of why, not just to your customers, but also to the employees who create the value for your customer, then the customer themself. The importance of your employees in understanding and creating "value" will become even clearer as we discuss the sixth organizing principle, associated with how.

YOU NEED MORE THAN ONE HERO

Another thing that nine of the top ten crime shows of the 1990s shared was their dependence on only one or two lead characters. These shows revolved around these lead characters for the entire length of the series. This same dynamic is true for most small businesses.

But do they have to be the same actors? For example, the show Law & Order remained relevant, even as its cast members came and went over its twenty-year run. They did continue to hold onto some long-running main characters, such as Steven Hill as District Attorney Adam Schiff (seasons 1-10), Jerry Orbach as Detective Lennie Briscoe (seasons 3-14), S. Epatha Merkerson as Lieutenant Anita Van Buren (seasons 4-20), Sam Waterston as Executive Assistant District Attorney (later District Attorney) and Jack McCoy (seasons 5-20), yet no one actor performed in all twenty seasons.

Dick Wolf, the creator of the show, was able to make significant cast changes by staying true to a winning formula, one that was not dependent on any single character. While some characters and the actors who portrayed them changed, the key positions played by the majority of actors remained constant.

WHAT THAT MEANS TO YOUR BUSINESS

The equivalent for your business is to maintain a strong reliance on your customer value proposition, strategic style and business culture. If these three elements are securely in place, your business operation, and the outcome it produces, will be far less reliant on any one person.

Yet—when you get your people right, you are best positioned to articulate how each employee contributes to the value created in each of the products and services you provide, at a price that earns you a profit.

> **...when you get your people right, you are best positioned to articulate how each employee contributes to the value created in each of the products...**

The stronger the culture of cooperation and collaboration, the more the team members will buy in to your company. When you have team members competing against each other it can cause friction, backbiting and subtle sabotage. Employees who work in "great" companies say that you can trust the people you work for, enjoy the people you work with, and believe in the product you sell.

> *"There are two ways of being creative.*
>
> *One can sing and dance*
>
> *Or one can create an environment in which singers and dancers flourish."*
>
> **WARREN BENNIS**

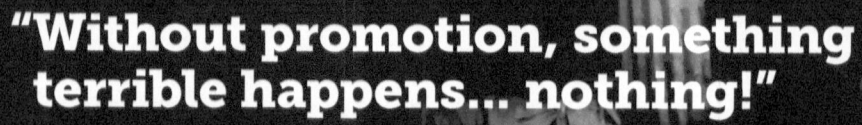

"Without promotion, something terrible happens... nothing!"

P.T. Barnum
American Showman and Businessman
SJuly 4, 1810 - April 7, 1891

CHAPTER EIGHT

6th ORGANIZING PRINCIPLE: HOW?
Promotions and Packaging

At any given time, only a small to very small percentage of consumers will have a genuine need or desire for your products. I know that hurts, doesn't it? To entice them to buy from you, you must succinctly articulate the benefits the buyer will receive. The best way to do this is to work forward from "the problem your product solves" to identify precisely why the customer should want to buy from you over your competitor.

Your unique selling proposition (USP) is what differentiates your business from your competitor's. It can be just a few targeted statements that reflect the real and perceived benefits of your goods and services; but—these must be unique to your business. Your goal is to present your buyer with clear reasons to buy from you, rather than anyone else.

> *...many business leaders will try to "hang in there," if they have enough revenue to skimp along for months, or even years. But they're tenaciousness is ultimately futile...*

The greater the number of similar businesses or products available, the higher the competition for your target customer's attention. As the uniqueness of your message and product decreases, the noise level and chaos will increase, resulting in a never-ending fight for customer sales. For most businesses, this dynamic is a slow killer. Sadly, many business leaders will try to "hang in there," if they have enough revenue to skimp along for months, or even years. But they're tenaciousness is ultimately futile.

YOUR OWN USP

How can you can minimize your risks in a crowded marketplace? You begin by determining the true value you provide to your customers, by focusing on what is unique and different about the products or services you provide. Your USP needs to accurately differentiate you from competing brands, and give your buyer a clear, logical reason to prefer your business to your competitor's.

Failure to define and communicate your USP in a clear, concise and compelling manner is essential to your business's success. True, you can remain on the endless treadmill of working really hard, but getting little, if anything, in return.

Many business leaders will do the necessary hard work to discover a point of differentiation, but then "blow it" by failing to communicate that point in a clear, concise and compelling message.

TARGET CUSTOMER
Has dollars to spend on a problem that needs to be solved or a want served.

THE QUESTION BECOMES
Who? What? When? Where? and Why?

BREAK THROUGH THE NOISE

PURCHASE TRANSACTION
Occurs because they chose to buy from YOU to solve their problem over buying from someone else or not buying at all

DIALOGUE WITH CUSTOMERS

The solution is to engage in dialogue, not monologues, with your customers. These dialogues must take place in your customers' language. If they speak Spanish, learn to speak Spanish, not Greek. Listen to the words your customers use, then reflect their words right back to them. They'll know you're hearing them, loud and clear.

To more easily communicate your USP to your customers, keep the following three points in mind:

1. **Be clear**. If your customers aren't clear about who you are, what you stand for and what value you bring to them, they aren't going to bring you their business.

2. **Be concise**. If you're somewhat clear, but tend to go on and on with your message, your customer will "tune out" your static noise, and take their business to someone who gets directly to the heart of what matters: the problem they are trying to solve.

3. **Be compelling.** Use your words to persuade your customers to take action. It's the best way to position yourself for a sale. With a compelling message, no "luck" is necessary.

BE CAREFUL OF INDUSTRY BUZZ WORDS

It's risky to base your promotional message on information derived directly from your employees. These individuals are predisposed to correctly interpret the messages you're communicating, and accept it. They also speak in "buzz words" that people in the industry understand, but regular people do not find as familiar. Employees and staff definitely cannot be considered to be "average consumers" of that product category.

Those who work for you will spend more time thinking about your product in one afternoon than the average consumer will in a lifetime. The key is in being able to succinctly articulate, in three to five statements, what problem your product solves for the buyer, and how they benefit from what you offer. Ultimately, you must be able to communicate this message clearly to anyone, including those who don't recognize that there is a solution for their problems.

PROMOTION

I define promotion as the advancement of a product or service, through publicity (earned media) and/or advertising (paid media), to promote the sale of a commercial product or service. To communicate an effective promotional message, you must be able to answer the following questions:

TABLE 5	
What do you have to say?	Message
Who needs to hear it?	Audience
Where are you going to say it?	Medium
How are you going to say it?	Words and Graphics (execution) that entertains, engages and informs

Advertising campaigns fail because businesses communicate the wrong message, or they communicate it to the wrong audience, or a combination. The insights shared in this chapter are aimed at helping you get your message right. Let's take a minute to review some of the factors we've already learned that are important in communicating an effective message.

The insights you developed in Chapter 3, associated with who, helped you to define your target customer. In Chapter 5, you identified when your target customer is most-likely to be open to your message; in Chapter 6, you identified where you would most-effectively communicate this information; in Chapter 7, you identified the why, which is the noble purpose for your employees and the reason your business exists.

If your employees don't believe in the noble purpose for your business, then it will prove impossible for them to communicate how the product or service will benefit your customer. You are better able to get your staff on your team working toward shared goals when you help them feel "ownership" in the great business you are building.

DEFINING YOUR PROMOTIONAL MIX

The specific combination of promotional methods you incorporate to communicate your message to your target audience defines your promotional mix. Your promotional mix may include the mediums of personal selling, print or broadcast advertising, direct marketing, signage and/or merchandising. This is why the heavy lifting necessary to determine the who, what, when, where, and why for your business is a never-ending pursuit.

The size of your promotion investments is shaped by your sales goals and the degree of awareness that already exists for your product. You can make your promotion dollars work more effectively for you when you think in terms of which element in the marketing mix represents the best marketing lever to promote your product or service.

The success of your promotional investments is also driven by how well your messaging represents what is most important for your target customer to learn about your business. If you fail to communicate how you can help them solve a problem, they aren't likely to read your message or retain the information. If they don't retain your message, the only sales you will make will be "impulse sales," because your promotions will have no staying power.

Your promotions only influence behavior when they are relevant to your target customer. In contrast, when your promotions are irrelevant, they will have no influence on behavior. You are already committed to what you are doing. It's the prospective customer who needs your help to move along the following purchase decision funnel, as they become informed, and then influenced, through your promotions.

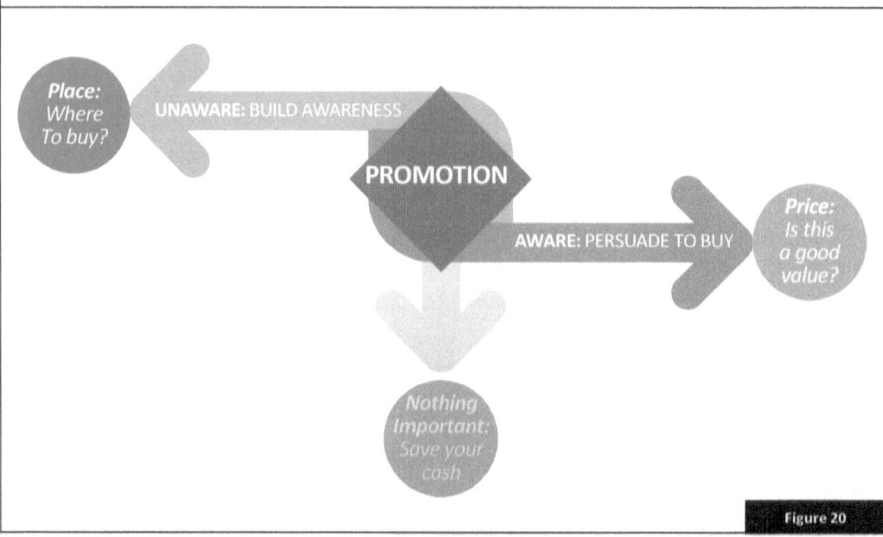

Figure 20

THE GOAL IS "AMOR" (TO LOVE) YOUR PRODUCT

Your typical target customer will never move from "awareness" to "buy" in one big leap. (Only the impulse buyer will do this.) Once the target customer becomes aware, they will begin to consider your product or service. If you are successful in creating enough interest, then they may begin to shop. If you fail to create this initial interest, they will hold back in proceeding to seek further information, or they may stop at this point, because they are not seeing enough of a reason to continue to shop.

The goal of your promotions is to keep your target audience inquiring continually, until they become a customer. An inquiring mind is open to buying. The minute your customer thinks they have enough information to correctly determine the value of the product or service, they will stop inquiring and move on to making a "buy" or "pass" purchase decision.

Your goal is to get your customers to love how the product or service they bought from you delivered on its promise. In Spanish, "amor" means to love. When your customers amor your product they are more likely to buy "a more" from you.

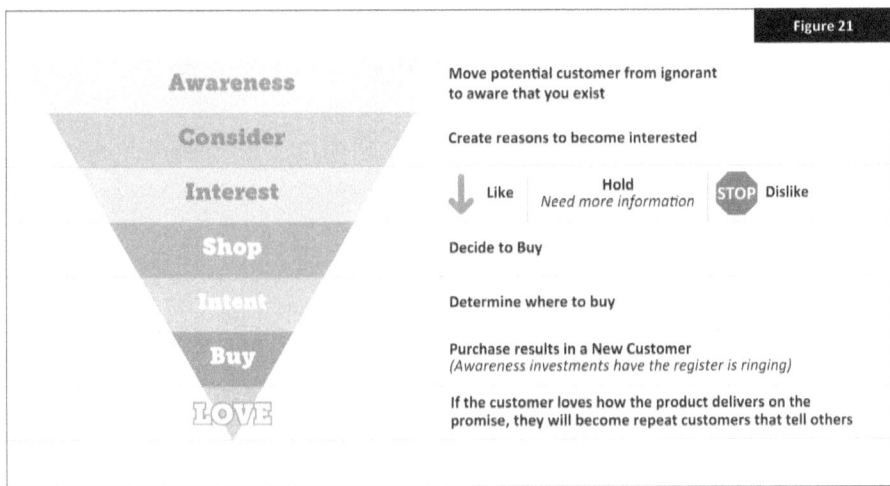

Figure 21

CALL TO ACTION

Once a customer begins to shop, they've already determined that they are open to buying. The question is where to buy? Consumer behavior is best influenced when you are engaging the customer in a "call to action" that shapes their intent. The intent you are trying to create leads them to determine where they can buy from you.

Building a "powerful visual brand" through intense advertising isn't likely to be within the marketing budgets of most small businesses. Brand building is for companies with oversized marketing budgets.

A good rule of thumb regarding your marketing budget is to invest at least half of your promotion dollars on your most-effective media. This means, that you have to know how your target customer is connected to you, so that you can lead with your best hand. I'm not a poker player, and yet even I know I'm not going "all in" with a pair of deuces. It's important to develop a clear strategy before spending those limited advertising dollars.

SPEAK THEIR LANGUAGE

By itself, promotion is not very useful. It must be directly related to what the target customer most values. For me, it's best to base an effective promotion on what is clearly new or different about your business. It has to be important enough for you to spend money communicating a focused message to your customers.

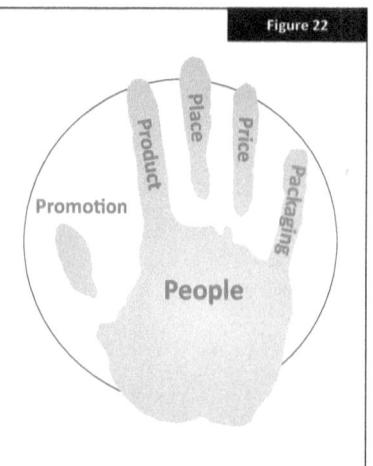

Figure 22

Your promotion goal is to tell your target how you will deliver on what they value. If you don't have anything new to promote to your customers, then direct your promotions toward the area of key interest for your target customer, and create the motivation for them to try the product or service you offer.

To review, you will improve the effectiveness of your promotions when you speak to your target customer in compelling and relevant terms.

Anchor your messages on the marketing mix elements most important to the customer. Here's a hint: Think about the importance of your thumb in gripping an object. The function of the thumb is to work with the other digits. Your promotions are like your thumb; they need to work with the most important elements in your marketing mix, to help influence people to buy from you.

You move the customer through the purchase funnel, from awareness to buy, when your promotions offer one clear, specific, memorable benefit. The success of your promotions is closely proportionate to the purpose of your message. People don't necessarily care about you or your business; they care about solving their problems. Your message must point out, identify or focus on what they might want from you and how it can help solve this problem.

Business success often comes down to communicating the right message to the right people at the right time. As you think about your promotional needs, consider which element of the marketing mix is most important for your promotional emphasis.

Below is a short list of the most common elements, categorized by the marketing mix, that you might want your business to be known for: Just as you use your thumb to grip

Table 6			
PRODUCT	**PLACE**	**PACKAGING**	**PRICE**
Quality	Retail	Protect Product	List Price
Features	Wholesale	Product Identification	Discounts
Benefits	Direct Sales	How to Use Info	Payment Period
Service/Support	eCommerce	Point of Sale	Credit Terms
Warranty	Distribution	Merchandising	Bundling

something important to you, your promotions need to support the most important element of your marketing mix, which is the one most important to your target customer. If you message too broadly, because you can't decide what is most important to say, you will only confuse people.

CONSISTENT COMMUNICATION

Let's take a look at who is ultimately communicating these promotional messages: your employees. One of the surest ways to flush your cash down the toilet is when your employees aren't buying into what you are promoting.

A disappointed customer won't come back, nor will they refer you to others.

As I've mentioned previously if you are saying "X" and your employees are delivering "Y," you have an unavoidable "disconnect" which will nearly always disappoint your customer and frustrate your employees, at the same time. A disappointed customer won't come back, nor will they refer you to others. An angry customer will often tell everyone within earshot about his or her horrible experience with your business.

In contrast, when your employees know the why behind what they do, negative customer experiences will decline. In the U.S. government study on "Why Customers Stop Buying," we learned that 68% of your customers stop buying from you because they feel that your employees don't care about them or their business. You can correct for this by cultivating employees who believe in your promotions, and in the products and services they are paid to deliver, and who consistently value and provide quality service to your customers.

ANOTHER CRIME SHOW

One of my favorite crime shows from the 1990s was Matlock, a legal drama starring Andy Griffith in the title role of criminal defense attorney Ben Matlock. The Fred Silverman Company, Dean Hargrove Productions, Viacom Productions, and Paramount Television produced the show. The show originally aired through the 1986 to 1992 seasons on NBC, and then moved to ABC through its 1995 season.

The show's winning format borrowed from the how established by Perry Mason, on CBS, with Matlock identifying the perpetrators and then confronting them in dramatic courtroom scenes. The difference in how with Mason was his ability to get his clients free at a pretrial hearing, whereas Matlock secured their acquittal at trial. Ben was adept at bringing the actual perpetrator to the witness stand, where he masterfully questioned them and shrewdly exposed the truth of their crimes.

In my opinion, the how is what makes a show unique, and it's the thing that keeps the viewers tuning in every week. If the how is suddenly changed, you run the risk of losing your audience. For instance, if a new, rogue writer suddenly decided that Matlock should take the law into his own hands in an episode and execute his own brand of justice outside the confines of the courtroom, viewers would be jolted. There would be a "disconnect" from the established and successful formula of the show—and you can bet that network executives would be calling to find out who they should fire.

*If the **"how"** is suddenly changed, you run the risk of losing your audience.*

SIX PRINCIPLES SO FAR

We have discussed six organizing principles thus far. Violating any one of these in isolation may not necessarily prove fatal for your business. It is the cumulative violation of an organizing principle that can turn it into a "fatal flaw"—particularly when the violation results in failing to attract customers who will buy from you at a price that earns you profit. It's basic Business 101.

The last organizing principle I'll share with you is the most important of the seven organizing principles for owning a great business. The big problem is that you can be darn near perfect in the other six we've discussed, but you'll still go out of business if you fail to master the seventh, crucial organizing principle: making a profit, by charging the right price.

"No man has a right to expect to succeed in life unless he understands his business, and nobody can understand his business thoroughly unless he learns it by personal application and experience."

P.T. BARNUM

CHAPTER NINE

7th ORGANIZING PRINCIPLE: PROFITS?
Price

Your business needs profits to justify its continued existence. You may have already identified the 5 W's + H aligned to the 6 Ps in marketing for your business, but none of these factors really matters if you don't make a profit. At the end of the day, your profit per transaction trumps all other metrics.

Put another way, you can only sell so many products or provide so many services at a loss before you have no money remaining to fund your operations. When you're out of cash, you're out of business. It's straight from Accounting 101.

Selling anything at a loss can mean one of two things: Either the buyer does not appreciate the value you are creating for them, or you are not efficiently producing and delivering your product. Either way, there is no exchange of value happening. There is no need being served or want being satisfied. You are losing out on this transaction.

EXCHANGE CASH FOR VALUE

The dollars you earn for your products and services reflect the consideration given in exchange for the transfer of ownership, from your business to the buyer. As the foundation of a commercial transaction, price is determined by the amount the buyer is willing to pay, and the amount the seller is willing to accept.

Price is the only element in the marketing mix that actually brings in money. The other elements of product, place, promotion, packaging and people are the investments you make in order to get people to pay your price.

You have to invest in your people and your means of production and distribution before you can deliver a product or service of value that someone will want to buy. It's "your cost of doing business." The key is in being able to charge a price for your products and services that is greater than your costs, so that each transaction generates a profit.

CIRCULATE CASH IN THE COMMUNITY

The simple truth is, the more you can bring in for your products and services, the more money you will have to cover your expenses. When you have money left over, you have a profit. When you don't, you have a loss. This is a business law—because ultimately, every business is a success is as simple as that.

The only way you can survive losses on your sales is when you have substantial cash reserves in the bank. Otherwise, your revenues must always be greater than your expenses, or you will soon be out of business. Your business is not just important for you and your loved ones. The circulation of cash keeps the economy of your community, state and nation going strong. The more you bring in to your business, the more you will have to share with employees, staff and to invest in expanding your business.

If you have enough cash to sustain operations for any length of time, you can absorb a loss on each sale. But why would you want to? I will never understand why anyone would pay people to do business with them, unless it's in the earliest stages of starting up your business.

If you're like me, you're likely to be working too hard to subsidize your customers' purchases from you. This is why you need to know what the market will bear, in order to determine whether you can charge a high enough price to cover your costs.

LOWER COST OR INCREASE VALUE

In any transaction, you will likely to be higher or lower in price than someone else. When it comes to price, you have only two viable levers to work with. You can increase the benefits to increase the value for your customer, or you can decrease your price. Either way, you are increasing value. But think about what kind of value you want to create.

If your target customer tells you that you are too expensive, you have either failed to effectively communicate the benefits, or you are competing against a more operationally efficient business. This does not dismiss the reality that there are some people who are only happy when they are able to negotiate a deal. When that happens ask them "What do you think is a fair price for the value I am giving you?"

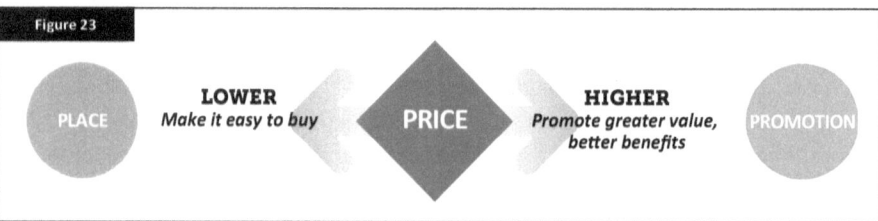

Figure 23

The key is to earn the right to increase your price, by clearly providing greater benefits to your customers, so they will prefer to bring their business to you. This is achieved when you provide more of what your customer wants, without a substantial increase in the cost of delivery. The best way to do this is to solve an irritation or remove a potential fear.

As your customer approaches the decision to buy from you, any fear or insecurity that arises makes it harder for them to connect to the value you are creating for them. This fear only disappears completely when they gain confidence in your solution to their problem.

You can do a lot to help your customers overcome the fear of doing business with you. How? By creating clarity and precision around who they are, what they need, when they need it, and where they will find it.

Here's a quick graphic that simply illustrates the PRICE/VALUE equation:

YOUR TEAM CREATES THE VALUE

You make superior value connections with your customers when your employees understand the why and your customers see how your business is unique. Providing clear answers to these questions allows you to set, and

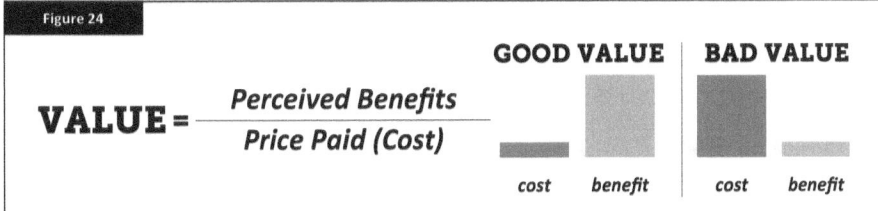

Figure 24

maintain, a price for your products and services that provides a good value to the customer and a profit for you.

No one wants to incur a cost greater than the benefit they derive. When establishing prices, you can avoid being seen as a bad value by either increasing benefits or decreasing costs to increase perceived, or real value to the customer. When you know what people perceive to be of value, and your employees understand how to deliver that value cost-effectively, you are owning a great business.

FAIR PRICING

In my business, I want to offer my customers fair pricing. I don't want to charge the highest price, nor do I want to give my products away. By charging fair prices for the value my business creates, we are making price less important, and we're then able to move the customer on to the what, when and where considerations.

For the buyer, the value of a product depends on their perception of the price they paid and the benefits they received, from their purchase. The price paid in a transaction is not only financial. It may involve other things that a buyer must be willing to give up.

For example, in addition to paying cash, a customer may have to spend time learning to use a product, pay to have an old product removed from their home or office, or temporarily close down their current operations while a product is being installed; or they might have to incur other expenses.

These additional costs, beyond the actual price they pay for the transfer of ownership, can be very real, or they can be seen as "opportunity costs." In economic terms, "opportunity cost" is what a person sacrifices in choosing one option over another. Opportunity costs are defined as the value of the "next best alternative." The item that you don't choose is the opportunity cost. It is a measure of the sacrifice we make when we are forced to make choices.

In my business, I often see repeat customers wrestle with this issue. Through past experience, they have already shopped and bought from us on other projects, so they are not seriously considering a competitor. The question they are still wrestling with is should they pay us, do it themselves, or do without?

> **What I have seen more often than not, though, is a serious underestimation of the time and skill level required to do it yourself, successfully...**

As a businessman, I appreciate the problem of tight cash flow. I also appreciate the concept of "doing it yourself," especially if you have the time and the skill, but not the money. What I have seen more often than not, though, is a serious underestimation of the time and skill level required to do it yourself, successfully. Over the years, I have spent more money "doing it myself" than I would have paid a professional to do the work. The concept of "opportunity costs" is one of the most important concepts we learn in economics.

Price affects demand. Higher prices decrease the demand for any product or service. When the price of an item or service is high, individuals must consider that buying the item may prevent them from purchasing another, more valuable item. As result, the opportunity cost of the item under consideration may be seen as too high. And this will result in less demand for that item, at that price point.

SUPPLY AND DEMAND

Another important economic concept is the Law of Supply & Demand. It's highly relevant to our understanding of price, value and profits, yet it is often overlooked. In 1767, in *The Wealth of Nations*, Adam Smith generally assumed that the supply price was fixed, but that its "merit" (or value) would decrease as its "scarcity" increased. In effect, Smith identified how the unit price for a particular good varies, until it settles at a point where the quantity demanded by consumers approximately equals the quantity supplied by producers, at a particular price, which results in an economic equilibrium for price and quantity. The challenge is the marketplace rarely achieves economic equilibrium. Figure 27 shows the four basic laws of supply and demand that exist when you don't have price/quantity equilibrium.

I believe that it's impossible to do great business in a world that is at economic equilibrium for price and quantity. And because I believe this I want to illustrate exactly how supply and demand function in the marketplace.

If supply is tight for your particular product and demand is high for similar products, you will have the opportunity to earn higher profits. Unfortunately, you'll also face the risk of new competitors entering this attractive market. Personally, I have never competed in this type of market, but it does exist.

When supply is high and demand is low, you will find yourself engaged in a price battle. Most businesses operate in this type of market, in which the winners are often those with the lowest costs of production. This is the market I compete in with Design Dynamics.

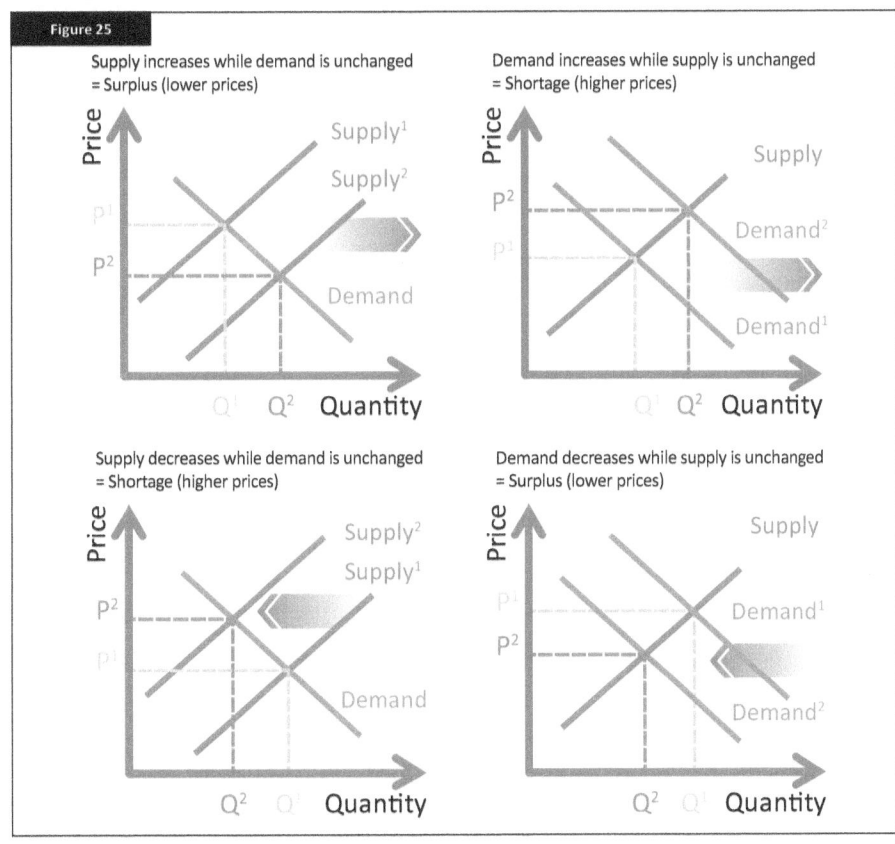

Figure 25

The recognized drivers of supply as a determiner of price are:
1. The production costs: how much does the item cost to produce
2. The technology used in production, and its rate of advancement
3. Your knowledge of and expectations about future prices
4. The number of suppliers that exist in the current market

The recognized drivers of demand as an influencer of price are:
1. The income levels of those buying
2. The prices of related goods and services
3. The consumers' expectations about future prices and incomes
4. The number of potential customers

MAINTAIN PROFIT

How do you know, without a doubt, that you are violating the seventh organizing principle in business? It's when you are unable to maintain a profitable business model with a proven revenue stream.

Failing to clearly and precisely define your who, what, when, where and why in the light of the 6 Ps as they relate to earning a profit will sink your business. What makes owning your own business so difficult is that you can actually have each of the 5 W's + H solved, but still lose your business if you are failing to earn profits.

If you're a startup, you need to move swiftly and do it without spending too much cash, as you figure out your recipe for success, or you will be out of business almost before you've begun. An error too many start ups do is to hire employees before they really need them. The more you can do yourself or hire independent contractors when needed, the more you can maintain profit.

> *...you need to move swiftly and do it without spending too much cash, as you figure out your recipe for success...*

If you're an established business, you still need to think and move quickly if you are going to remain profitable. Your key is to experiment and refine. Think "fail fast," if you're going to fail at all, as you continue to refine and fine-tune what you have to do to nail down your profit model.

VALUE, REGULAR, AND PEAK PRICING

The Walt Disney theme parks represent one of the best examples of the Law of Supply and Demand. They've really got this down. In February, 2016, they announced new variable pricing, which would be instituted at different times of the year for their U.S. theme parks. They came to this decision after polling park guests about their visits, with the goal to better even-out the demand, amid growing attendance.

The results of their research led Disney to institute a new pricing model, effective immediately on their announcement, for visitors to Disneyland and Walt Disney World. The new pricing model that resulted ranged from a 4% discount from current prices, to a 20% increase, depending on when each park was visited.

The move created three sets of prices: "value," "regular" and "peak." These categories are expected to correlate to weekdays (value); weekends and summer weekdays (regular); and holiday periods and summer weekends (peak).

For example, at Disneyland, in Anaheim, California, the regular adult price of $99 a day has changed to $95 on value days, $105 on regular days, and $119 on peak days. At Walt Disney World's Magic Kingdom, in Orlando, Florida, adult price value tickets are now $105, the same price as the previous single-day admission. Regular-period tickets are now $110 and peak period, $124.

One of Disney's key measures of success is their 70% return rate for first time visitors. Knowing this metric allows them to raise prices to decrease demand when necessary: They know it's very likely that the visitors they do have will come back. Their visitors' love reliving the Disney experience is what gives Disney the luxury of having a highly favorable, demand-driven pricing model.

DEMAND DRIVEN MODEL

Wouldn't we all love to see this in our own businesses? Yes, but don't lose sight of the fact that Disney has been at this since July 17, 1955. They have had sixty years to work their magic. The other thing to appreciate about Disney is they never rest solely on their current success; they are always pushing themselves to offer an even-better experience on your next visit to one of their theme parks.

While implementing a highly favorable, demand-driven pricing model like Disney's isn't likely to be possible for most of our businesses, it doesn't mean we still can't do great business.

The key is in learning to unlock the seven organizing principles that will make your business a great business. Your business is built on selling a product or service to people who have a need you can serve or a want you can satisfy. Your focus is on solving a problem. The bottom line for all business dealings is to shape your offer at a price that earns you a profit.

This means you must personally be 100% accountable for the decisions you make and actions you take; if you fail to hold yourself accountable, any value you create for your customers will come about by chance, and you will never maximize your profits.

CRIME SHOW EXAMPLE

One popular TV show I was not drawn into was the 80's hit, Miami Vice. However, I did enjoy watching Don Johnson in Nash Bridges (CBS, 1996-2001), a show created by Carlton Cuse and produced and filmed on location in San Francisco. The show employed several hundred local workers, including production crews and staff members, carpenters, electricians, set designers, grips, set dressers, props, scenic artists, location managers, costumers, drivers, cameramen, special effects, soundmen, makeup and hair stylists and production assistants. As a result of these high production costs, each episode of the series cost nearly $2 million to produce.

Even though Nash Bridges obtained fair Nielsen ratings and generated enough interest from CBS to renew it for a seventh season, the show was canceled.

Paramount Network Television, the show's producers, felt that its $2 million/episode production cost was just too much, and they were no longer willing to pay this enormous cost.

What's interesting is that, at the time, Viacom owned both CBS and Paramount. CBS and Paramount knew that they had produced 122 episodes, more than enough to put the series into syndication—and that made the decision to end the show even easier.

Helping people buy the things they need is one of the most satisfying parts of leading a business. Connecting people with the products you make and the services you provide becomes more difficult when you're in the dark on any one of the seven organizing principles for doing great business.

> **Helping people buy the things they need is one of the most satisfying parts of leading a business...**

Particularly, when your revenues aren't covering your costs.

When the profit principle is violated, you are exposing your underbelly to the most fatal flaw for any business. You're violating the most basic law of business: when you run a business without profits, your ability to deliver any value evaporates, and your business will not survive.

This is how you make sure that your business is in the 50% who succeed and are great. You now know some of the pitfalls to watch for and metrics to manage by. Your profit principle will guide you in decision making and hiring staff.

"We have an infinite amount to learn both from nature and from each other."

JOHN GLENN

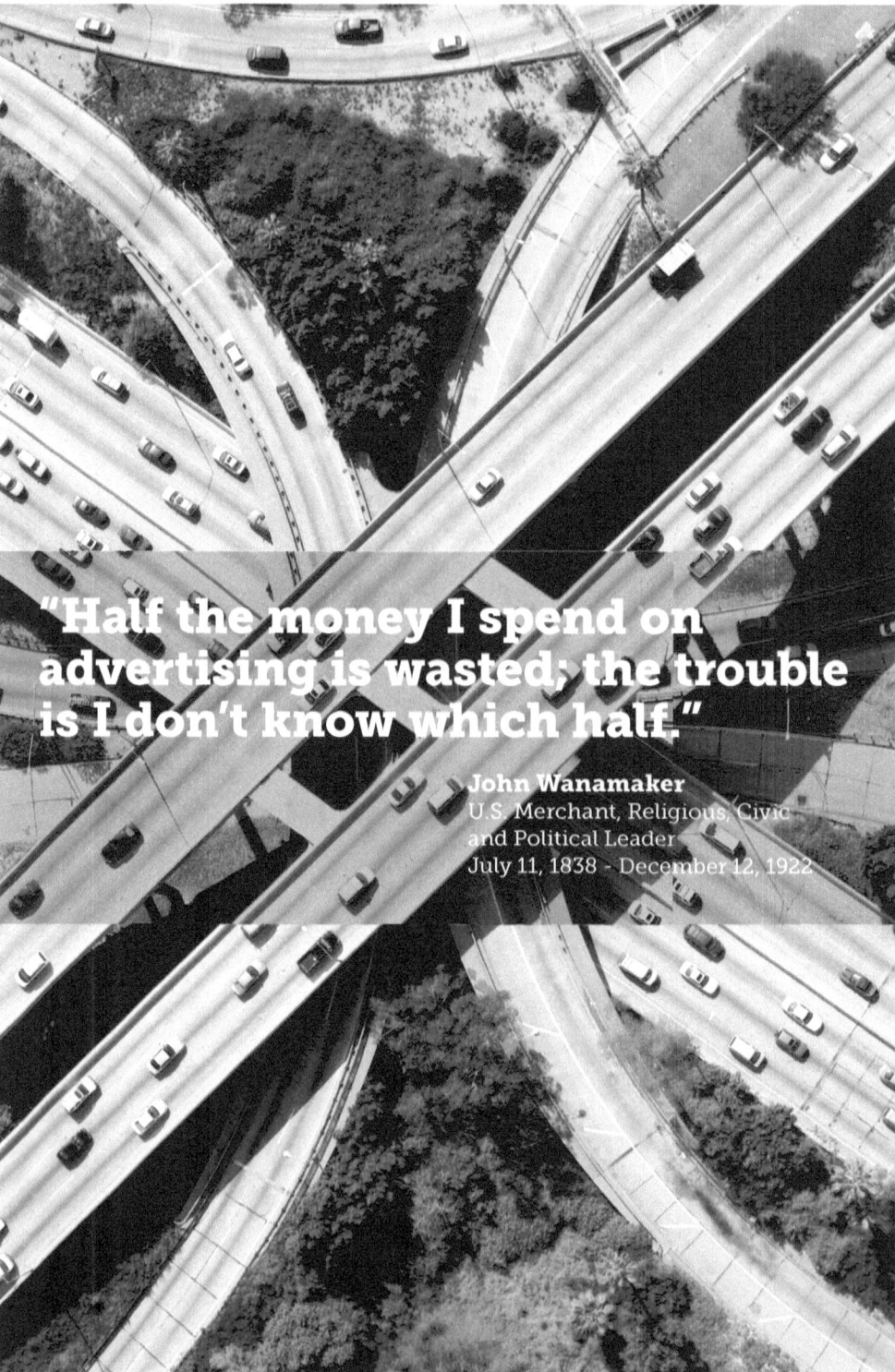

CHAPTER TEN

A FEW MORE NUGGETS OF WISDOM...

Over my career, I have worked for some poorly run businesses, and for some good Fortune 100 businesses, yet I've never worked for a great business. This is why, in 2009, I became a small business owner. My goal was at its core, to own a great business—both a great company to do business with and a great business to work for.

I know that I own a great business when my family, customers, and employees are thriving in their respective lives, because of their involvement with our company. This gives me tremendous satisfaction. A great business will be a win-win for everyone involved.

MOVING FROM GOOD, TO GREAT

In the book, *Good to Great*, Jim Collins discusses why some companies make the leap to greatness and others do not. When I read *Good to Great* in 2001, I was a member of the Nationwide Services Company leadership team. In my place of work, I found myself quickly agreeing with Collins' overarching theme that "good" is the enemy of "great."

In this follow-up book to his 1994 success *Built to Last*, Collins observes that the vast majority of companies never become great, because they become good enough, and that is the real problem. In his follow-up book, he focuses on the question, "What did these few good-to-great companies share in common, that distinguished them from comparable companies, who did not make this journey?"

Collins developed numerous valuable insights, including: "Level 5 Leadership," "First Who...Then What," "Confront the Brutal Facts (Yet Never Lose Faith)," and the "Hedgehog Concept," which leads to a "Culture of Discipline" and creates either a "Flywheel" or "Doomloop." These foundations of business thinking are important for every business leader who aspires to own a great business. If you haven't read *Good to Great*, I strongly encourage you to buy, and study, this book. Make it a permanent part of your business library.

GOOD THE ENEMY OF GREAT

The idea that good can be the enemy of great is the critical takeaway from this final chapter. In life, we have all faced the difficulty of understanding the difference between "knowing something" and "doing something." Effective doing requires discipline. It requires a willingness to put in the time and do the critical thinking necessary. Only then, once you have clearly laid out what needs to be done, can you execute it with determination.

Over my life, I have found it is easier to execute with confidence and determination when I know that I am working by a principle of truth. Remember, principles are "concentrated truth," packaged for application to a wide variety of circumstances. The 7-P Framework is intended to help you organize your thoughts into truths about your business, and then apply these truths in building a great business.

Reflect on the business you have worked for or have owned. Did they become complacent? Did they grow and evolve? Were the owners "just treading water" to stay afloat in an uneven economy?

Had you been in their shoes, what would you have done differently? Often, when we work for or with others, we learn not only what to do, but what not to do.

FINDING NEW CUSTOMER "GOLD"

As I was distributing the prototype for this book to a select group of book reviewers, an interesting challenge occurred at Design Dynamics. We experienced an immediate drop-off in business with our largest customer. The good news was that they hadn't stopped using us completely. The bad news was that their inventory levels were high, because they were experiencing their own unplanned drop-off in sales.

Their rapid purchasing adjustments had a ripple effect on us, causing us to make some immediate staffing-level adjustments. We did this through reduced hours, in order to preserve cash flow, while we worked even harder to find new customers and businesses to serve.

> *Existing customers are the veins of gold in your business goldmine. As long as the gold vein holds, business is good...*

Existing customers are the veins of gold in your business goldmine. As long as the gold vein holds, business is good. When the gold vein you depend on peters out, you find yourself working harder, for less and less, until you find your next vein of gold to mine.

THE NEVER-ENDING CHALLENGE

Eventually, all gold mines will run out of gold to mine, even those who were lucky enough to find the "mother lode." No "mother lode" is endless. And this key point is why gold mining companies spend so much money looking for their next pocket of gold to mine. It is a never-ending challenge to keep the pipeline of customers full.

What can you, as a business leader, learn from this? How could your business be doing things differently?

I stand behind my belief that the hardest thing to do in business is finding new customers, and I don't make this claim lightly. Over my career, I have worked in marketing and sales at PPG and VPI; in operations at Stater Bros Markets and Nationwide; and in human resources at Nationwide and VPI. I even did a stint as a financial controller while I was at Nationwide. And, since 2010, as the owner of Design Dynamics, I have had to manage all of the above.

In my long career, I found the easiest of my positions was HR, where my focus was on attracting, engaging and retaining our employees. The challenge in working with HR professionals is that they sometimes don't have the best business acumen. They can be somewhat territorial and they can often be risk-averse.

The second easiest function for me was Finance. Our most difficult monthly task was pulling the numbers together to perform our financial reporting and analysis. At first we were allotted two weeks to do month-end reporting. Then the CEO began asking to see the previous months' financial reports, only five days following the close of each month. His desire for faster reporting drove an unbelievably complex overhaul of our financial information management system (FIMS), which Nationwide spent millions to realize.

> *Everyone needs to know "who" the customer is, and "what" your company does to serve their needs or satisfy their wants.*

During my seven years in different staff functions, I always thought that we needed more direct exposure to our customers. Our functional leaders never shared this view of fewer layers between customer and management. I knew of many people at Nationwide and at PPG, who had never had a single direct conversation with a paying customer, in their career. Even in these billion dollar companies, this should never happen. Everyone needs to know "who" the customer is, and "what" your company does to serve their needs or satisfy their wants.

TOUGH CHOICES

How to stay true to work process and still connect with customers is one of the toughest choices in business. During my years in operations, the challenge has always been to balance operational efficiency with customer demand. In order to provide the best value to your customers, you need your operations to have process discipline.

The disconnect occurs when your target customer's needs don't align cleanly and efficiently with your established workflows and operating procedures. It's like asking for water from the moon. Stop and think—should you hijack your work process to meet the needs of the customer, or should you turn the customer away by telling them that you can't meet their needs because it is outside your company's scope?

Any changes to written, or unwritten, policies still require a series of decisions to be made, including deciding who will make them. The more hoops I was forced to jump through, the harder I found it to retain valued customers.

Highly bureaucratic organizations make it so tough for the people on the frontline to accommodate the customer that they simply give up, and fall back to toe only "company policy," so they don't put their jobs at risk. This is why it is becoming harder and harder to experience great customer service.

I am not saying that every customer demand should be honored. But I am saying that sometimes very reasonable requests could and should be honored, even if it means going that extra mile. Yet they are not because employees do not feel empowered to do what is in the best interest of the customer, and ultimately, their company and their own careers. In your pursuit of a great business remember it must be a win for everyone concerned. Create a culture that helps staff to be "problem solvers" and invested in the business and the community.

GROWING YOUR BUSINESS

When it comes to growing your sales, there are only three fundamental growth strategies to execute. You can either go after more new customers, get more money from existing customers or win back lost customers. No matter what terms you use to describe your revenue enhancing efforts, they will fall into one of the following three strategies:

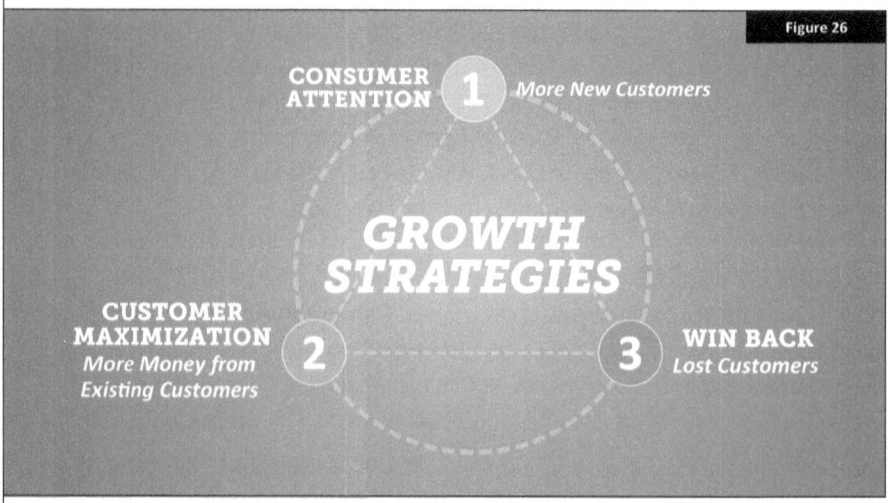

Figure 26

When everyone involved in executing your growth plan is clear about which fundamental strategy you are trying to execute, you will improve your probabilities of success in growing your business. Below is a breakdown of the three fundamental growth strategies, from easiest to hardest in execution.

CUSTOMER MAXIMIZATION

My favorite theorem in geometry is "the shortest distance between two points is a straight line." Applying this logic to your customers, "the people who have bought from you in the past already know what solutions you offer and where to connect with you."

Existing customers represent the shortest distance to higher sales. This is why repeat customers are so important to your business. Straight-line transaction connections make up the easiest business your business will ever do. This is why getting more money from existing customers via "customer maximization" is the easiest growth strategy for your business.

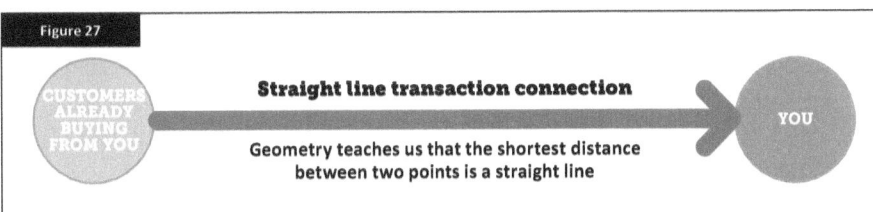

Customer maximization is about helping your valued customers realize their goals and aspirations over the life of the relationship they have with you. Maximization can only occur when you seek to truly understand who your customer is and what you can offer them. The straight line will only exist when what they buy from you next is of even greater value to them than what they have purchased from you in the past.

UP SELL OR CROSS SELL

Begin by identifying what additional products or services a particular customer could be buying from you that they are currently buying from someone else. The sales tactics employed here are often described as "up-selling" or "cross-selling."

Here's an example: Financial services companies are famous for wanting to become your one-stop source for all your financial needs. What they sometimes fail to realize is that just because I bank with them doesn't mean I will also allow them to manage my investments or insure my assets. Yet these companies continue to bombard me with their different financial product offerings because they are easily able to identify what it is that I'm not buying from them.

The typical cross-sell strategy of the financial services companies is a good demonstration of my next point: You will never maximize a customer through a one-size-fits-all approach, or by utilizing generic marketing promotions.

It's much more effective to deploy varying strategies that are highly personalized to your individual customers and their unique needs.

Simply put, mastering the seven organizing principles for owning a great business is your best strategy to use in preparing for a more-targeted customer maximization strategy. The key is in knowing what, exactly your customers most value about your business. Do they value the purchase itself? Or, do they value the longevity of the relationship, or other factors, such as the convenience of your location or the speed with which you can fulfill their order?

Once you determine this value source, you can then create the appropriate "hooks" for your best customers, and maintain your position as their supplier of choice. Your best hook lays in getting your existing customers to use a broader swath of your product portfolio. Knowing your customer inside and out is the only way to get there.

KNOW YOUR CUSTOMER

The challenge of customer maximization is to make sure that all of your customers' purchases add an acceptable level of profitability. I add this caution, because I've learned that in the spirit of being highly responsive to customer needs, it's easy to lose sight of what it's costing you to meet those important customer needs.

> **The challenge of customer maximization is to make sure that all of your customers' purchases add an acceptable level of profitability.**

You can guard against this by having a well-thought out matrix for all customer touch-points. These are the places where a customer is engaged by your product promotions or where they might be expected to make a purchase. Once you have identified these touch-points, you can map them out in a targeted plan to maximize top-line revenue and bottom-line profitability. It is only through effective management of these touch-points that can you achieve your customer maximization goals.

Amazon is a great example of a company succeeding through the strategy of customer maximization. There are many, many reasons why Amazon succeeds, yet I would argue that one of the most important is their obsession with keeping customers happy. Amazon carefully tracks all of its customers' previous orders, product searches, wish lists, shopping-cart contents, and returns. They even know how long its customer's cursor hovers over particular items. This allows Amazon to anticipate its customers' needs, even before its customers know them. It's a very, very effective strategy.

Tricia Duryee of Geek Wire posted on January 27, 2105, that Amazon's Prime members spend, on average, $1,500 per year, compared to $625 a year for non-members. Duryee pointed out, "initially, shoppers sign-up for Amazon Prime accounts to save on shipping costs, but they later find other appealing benefits, like free video, music streaming and book rentals on Kindle." Amazon Prime is a customer maximization strategy that predictably results in its members shopping more frequently, while buying more expensive items.

RETAINING VALUED CUSTOMERS

Existing customers are your most critical assets, yet few business leaders put forth the same effort to properly manage this asset that they do in the areas of finance and operations. Customer retention is the true backbone of business success. Everyone in your company, from the sales staff to the front-line customer service representatives, to the owner or CEO, should be concerned with customer relationship management and satisfaction.

> *Customer retention is the true backbone of business success.*

The customer is affected by every single interaction they have with your company. Failing to properly manage your customer assets extends far beyond the loss of the affected customer. Once the customer decides to walk away from your business, they are extremely hard to win back. The stark reality is that you are going to lose customers; the key question to identify is how are you losing them? The U.S. government study on "Why Customers Stop Buying" showed us that 68% of those customers, who stop buying from you, do so because they feel your employees don't care about them.

All employees, regardless of their primary job duties, are responsible for promoting and representing the business. I'll give you a quick example. In nursing school, a friend of mine was taught that every hospital employee is potentially responsible if a patient slips and falls on a wet floor: the person who caused the spill, the person who first saw it and didn't wipe it up, and the second and the third. You may think, "but it's the janitor's fault – he's the one with the mop." But the janitor was on another floor, cleaning up another spill. He was not even notified of this spill. Every one of the employees who knew of the spill and did nothing, is responsible; they were all empowered to provide a clean, safe environment for the hospital's "customers" (i.e. patients).

TIP OF THE ICEBERG

Any customer who feels that one of your employees doesn't care about their business represents the tip of the iceberg for serious problems in your business. Consider the sinking of the RMS Titanic. It all started near midnight on Sunday, April 14, 1912, in the North Atlantic Ocean, four days into the ship's maiden voyage from Southampton, England, to New York City. The Titanic was the largest passenger liner of its time, with an estimated 2,224 people on board. She struck an iceberg at 11:40 pm—and when she sunk two hours and forty minutes later at 2:20 am, more than 1,500 people would die—making it one of the deadliest maritime disasters in history.

During the day, the Titanic had received six warnings of sea ice, yet the crew failed to adjust her course. The Titanic's high speed in ice-filled waters was later criticized as reckless, but it reflected standard maritime practice at the time.

According to Fifth Officer Harold Lowe, the custom was "to go ahead and depend upon the lookouts in the crow's nest and the watch on the bridge to pick up the ice in time to avoid hitting it." Once again, like the example cited above: "It isn't my job. Someone else will do it."

The North Atlantic's ocean liners prioritized time-keeping above all other considerations, sticking rigidly to a schedule that would guarantee their arrival at an advertised time. Ships were frequently driven at close to their full capacity for speed, treating hazard warnings as advisories rather than as calls to action. In 1912, it was widely believed that ice posed little risk; close calls were not uncommon, and even some head-on collisions had not been disastrous.

Unfortunately for the Titanic, they did collide with an iceberg. While traveling 22 knots, near her maximum speed of 24 knots, lookout Frederick Fleet sighted the iceberg. Because of the size of the ship and the speed with which it was moving, the helmsman was unable to turn quickly enough to avoid the glancing blow that buckled her starboard (right) side and opened five of her sixteen compartments to the sea. The ships designers had designed the Titanic to stay afloat in the event that four of her forward compartments flooded, but they hadn't planned for the ship to stay afloat if any more compartments flooded. And so, on April 15, the Titanic sank—because one more compartment flooded than the vessel had been engineered for.

Consider Joseph Bruce Ismay, the English businessman who served as chairman and managing director of the White Star Line. He was the highest-ranking White Star official to survive the wreck of the company's brand new RMS Titanic. And for this circumstance, he was subject to severe criticism. Do you think Ismay would have liked the engineers to design the Titanic to stay afloat if five compartments flooded? Do you think he would have liked Captain Smith or Officer Murdoch to slow the ship down because of the sea ice warnings? Frederick Fleet did his job, spotting the iceberg, but unfortunately, not in time for the ship to change course. As a result, an avoidable tragic disaster occurred.

CUSTOMER CARE

When you have employees who cause customers to feel they don't care about their business, you have issues that need your immediate attention. Either you have people working for you who need to be bounced from your company, or you have procedures and processes, which are getting in the way of your employees taking great care of your customers. Sometimes the problem of not caring can be traced to the failure to provide your employees the tools they need to do a good job.

> *Sometimes the problem of not caring can be traced to the failure to provide your employees the tools they need to do a good job.*

For example, Frederick Fleet, the Titanic crewmen who spotted the iceberg, survived the sinking of the RMS Titanic. He was twenty-five years old when he was employed as a lookout aboard the Titanic. It was Fleet who first sighted the iceberg, ringing the bridge to proclaim, "Iceberg, dead ahead!" Frederick did his job as well as he could. Unfortunately, it was only learned during his testimony at the inquiries that followed that had he been issued binoculars, he would have seen the iceberg far in advance, because it was a highly visible blue iceberg, in calm seas, on a moonless night. Failure to give Frederick an important tool contributed to the tragedy of the Titanic.

PERSONAL EXAMPLE

My editor felt that the example from my own business that I am about to share should be deleted. Her concern was that because it happened so recently, that I would run the risk of it affecting my credibility. I chose to keep the following experience as an example of how important vigilance is in everything you do. Seemingly little things, like failing to give your lookout binoculars, can have damaging consequences.

...the back-breaker for me of this business failure was the feeling the customer had that we didn't care...

In the fall of 2015, while we were dealing with the order slowdown from our largest customer at Design Dynamics, we also suffered one of the biggest disappointments I've faced as a business owner. In the spring of 2012, we had won a $10,000/year account. We then lost that same customer in the fall of 2015. The contributing cause (or iceberg) of the customer loss was a missed due date on a complex project. Our failure to deliver this job on time caused the customer to review their experience with my company. Their conclusion was we didn't seem to care for their business.

I tried everything to change this outcome. I even went so far as to give the customer the graphics work we had completed at no charge, a $1,900 value, as a show of good faith, but the damage was done. The customer accepted the credit, but this did not change their decision about continuing to use us. While I hate losing a valued customer, the back-breaker for me of this business failure was the feeling the customer had that we didn't care.

I definitely did care. My employees on this project were too quick to accept the material sourcing issues we were working through. Without malice and the complete picture, they failed to keep the customer informed of our difficulties.

Sometimes there are certain factors outside of your control, as happened with this particular job. It happens with every business, everywhere in the world, at one time or another. Yet there is no excuse for my customer experiencing a sense of nonchalance, or no sense of urgency to correct or even offer an apology, from the two employees who had worked directly with this customer. Often, all that is required is a sincere apology and a promise to do better in the future. While the loss of this customer is still painful to me, it provided a definite learning opportunity for our employees, albeit a pricey training experience on what "not to do."

ATTRACTING NEW CUSTOMERS

Capturing new customers is the hardest and most expensive of the three growth strategies to execute. The "more new customers" strategy always begins with attracting their attention first. It is impossible to get a new customer until they know you exist. The inherent problem with awareness-building activities is that they cost money. The other problem is that, more often than not, your awareness-building investments fail to generate sufficient sales to cover the expense of the promotion.

> *Unless your business is "impulse based," you are constantly battling the "awareness" obstacle...*

This is why the John Wanamaker quote for the opening to this chapter is so appropriate, "Half the money I spend on advertising is wasted; the trouble is I don't know which half." In 1861, in partnership with his brother in-law, John Wanamaker opened his first store, in Philadelphia. In 1869, he opened his second store, capitalizing on his own name due to the untimely death of his brother-in-law, and renaming his business John Wanamaker & Co. In 1875, he purchased an abandoned railroad depot and converted it into a large retail store, called John Wanamaker & Co.

"The Grand Depot" was the first department store in Philadelphia. John was a creative innovator, a merchandising genius and proponent of the power of advertising. We still quote him on the challenge of advertising, because he identified an inherent challenge in promoting your business that is still true today.

In the eighth chapter, we discussed the sixth organizing principle, associated with how. This chapter showed you how important Promotion + Packaging decisions are to your business success. Unless your business is "impulse based," you are constantly battling the "awareness" obstacle. Remember, creating awareness is the first difficult step in capturing new customers.

PROSPECT OR SUSPECT

I use the terms "prospect" and "suspect" for those starting the sales process with me. Keeping that in mind, once a consumer is aware of your business, they will then become either a prospect or suspect as they begin to consider your product or service.

A prospect is someone who responds to your reasons why they should become interested in you. If they are interested in what you are promoting, they will begin to follow the "purchase decision funnel." (figure 21) If you fail to create interest or they stop engaging with you, it's because they aren't seeing reasons to consider your business further, and they return to being non-interested consumers. If they hold back for more information, and continue to keep after you for more and more information, they are more than likely a "suspect."

Suspects are people who meet my target customer criteria and who have indicated an interest in buying from our business. The challenges with suspects are they all start out looking like prospects, and yet never buy from us.

> *Interested sales prospects will engage with you consistently, while suspects will only engage with you as long as it's "safe..."*

They just take up my time, always wanting to learn more and more.

Like suspects, prospects also meet our target customer criteria. What's different is that they have indicated more than a passing interest in what we have to offer, by entering into and then continuing in a dialogue with us to learn more about how we can help them.

Suspects will give you permission to keep in touch with them, but they never become a serious prospect, one that you can convert into a customer. The problem with sales suspects is they don't wear a sign that says, "don't waste your time on me." To the contrary, they will behave in exactly the same ways that a sales prospect will. As a result, you will waste time, money and scarce resources trying to convince them to buy from you.

With care and thought, you can learn to develop indicator criteria, which differentiate prospects from suspects. One key way is to involve them in your sales process. Interested sales prospects will engage with you consistently, while suspects will only engage with you as long as it's "safe."

PROSPECTS WILL SHARE

Here's an easy way to separate a suspect from a prospect: ask them to share with you something about themselves or their business, perhaps something that is not publically known, and which will help you lead them to the best solution for their problem. Prospects who are genuinely interested in you and your product will usually see the value in sharing such information. Suspects will not.

Here's a quick example. If I'm trying to sell a new sign to you, and you're a serious prospect, you're going to share with me the critical information I need to know to best help you - like how much have you budgeted for your sign. Without this information, I am unable to accurately put together an effective solutions proposal for your benefit.

On the other hand, if you are merely a suspect, looking to find out what's on the market, you're going to be hesitant in providing this information. These are the consumers who you don't want to invest a lot of your limited time and resources in serving. Of course, you always want to be polite and approachable, and to project a professional image. But beyond this effort, it's best to redirect the suspect, and move on to the prospect. Sometimes it is a good practice to say "Perhaps you will be better served by..." Not everyone is a perfect fit for your business. When they do need your product, they will remember that you did not try to force sell them but referred them to someone else.

With suspects, it's about finding out if they have any interest in what you have to offer; whereas, with prospects, it's about further developing and defining that interest, as you work to turn them into customers.

As you learned in Chapter 8, the goal of your promotions is to keep your target audience inquiring until they become a prospect. You pursue this because an inquiring mind is open to buying.

The minute customers think they have all the information needed to make a determination of value; they will stop inquiring and move to making a "buy or pass" purchase decision.

> **Getting people to "buy" comes down to communicating with them in a way that meets their information needs not your promotion objectives**

Getting people to "buy" comes down to communicating with them in a way that meets their information needs not your promotion objectives. When people "pass," they have either tuned your message out or changed the channel on you. Either way they don't see the value in what you are selling and they have made the decision to keep their hard earned money from becoming yours.

SMALL ADJUSTMENTS-BIG IMPACT

One of my goals for this book is to give you small nuggets of wisdom that you can put into practice today. It has been my experience over my career, just as in my golf game; even a small adjustment can have a big impact.

As a small business owner and as a corporate executive, I have come to see something very clearly. Too many business leaders get caught up on what, while the marketing people are concentrating on the who, and the finance people are stuck on profits. All of them fail to realize and appreciate the investments needed to generate each of them.

I have learned that it is actually more about "the when". The when refers to the purchase decision "trigger" that leads someone to consider making a purchase. In my view, when is even more important than the who, in achieving the perfect definition of your target customer.

From the big-picture view, most everything you do in your business will key off of who or when, as reflected in the following figure:

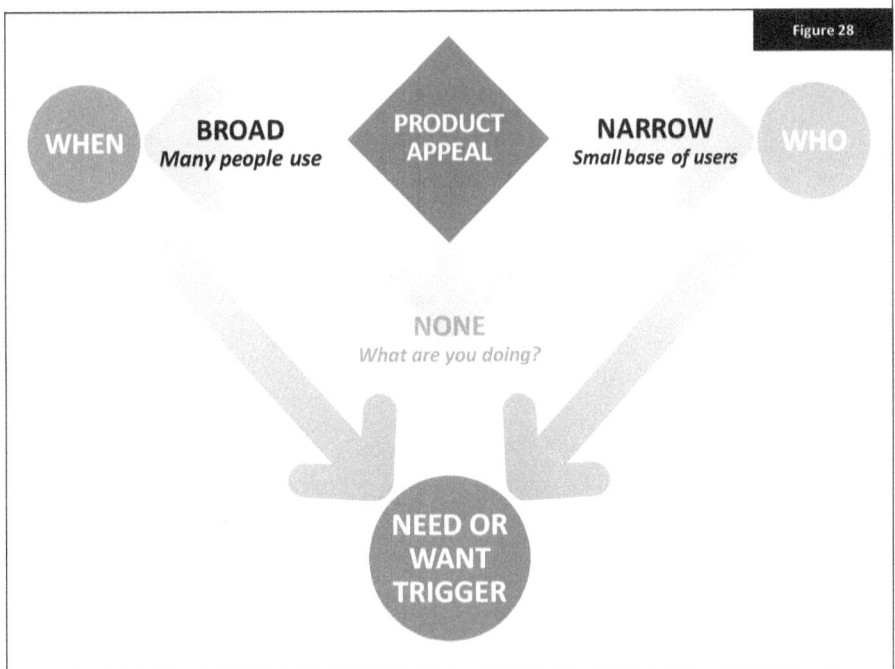

WHAT IS CUSTOMER'S TRIGGER

Before you put this book on your bookshelf, or loan it to someone else, please reflect on your customers. What triggers people to purchase products or services from your business. What is the deciding factor? The more precisely you understand the when that drives their decision to buy, the higher the probability you'll be able to repeat and refine the critical success factors for your business.

In real estate, it's location, location, and location. The same can be said of business. Do your customers know you and where to find you? Are they aware you may have the solution to their problem? If not, it becomes impossible for any exchange of value to occur. Even if people haven't bought from you yet, but they know about you, you're that much closer to a straight-line connection to a transaction. This is why large corporations spend millions on brand building, advertising and promotions.

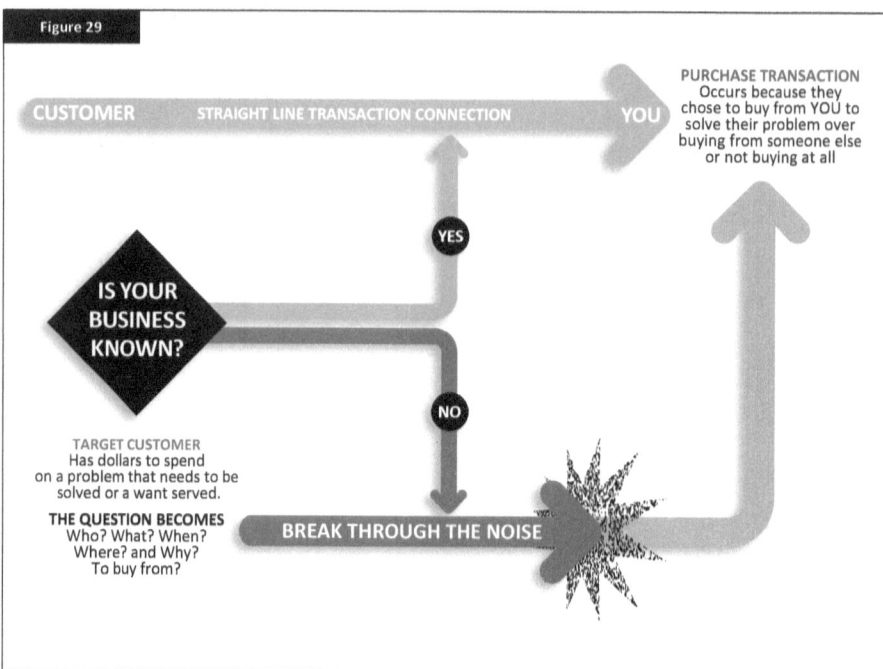

Figure 29

If your business has visibility and is well known, your problem then becomes one of helping your target customer see the value of your solution. They know you have a solution, but they need to gather enough information to determine if it represents the best value to them. And value can be a very individual thing: Maybe they value the speed of transaction. Or, maybe they have all the time in the world, and they value only the price. (Or, they might only value the product if it comes in the color pink.)

When your business is not well known, you have a combination of the noise of everyday life as well as the messages of your competitors blocking you from conducting any business transaction.

Once you become known, though, your problem becomes one of demonstrating value. This is why looking at the price/value equation for your product(s) is so important. When your perceived value is higher than the price you are charging, people are more likely to buy from you when you serve a need or satisfy a want that is important to them.

If the price you are charging is higher than the perceived value, people don't buy. They will buy from someone cheaper or lose sight of the need or want they have because you are charging more than they want to spend. This was our problem at PPG. We competed on a platform of product innovation, so our price/value equation was out of balance with the coil coaters who were competing on price.

YOUR TOP-LINE MATTERS

As I was finishing the first full draft of this book in May of 2015, Target and Walmart both had relatively new CEOs leading their respective companies. It was interesting to me at the time that both of these dominant retailers had shares which lagged behind the S&P 500 Retail index; yet, Target's shares were up 3.3% in 2015, while Walmart's shares were down 1.9%. This separation in performance was explained by the fundamentals for any business – Target was driving the top-line, and Walmart was not.

> *Unless you are drawing shopping traffic that translates into sales transactions you will struggle...*

The top-line is one place where short-sighted financial wizards can put you at risk, by over-emphasizing cost-cutting and financial engineering. You can't save your way to success. Unless you are drawing shopping traffic that translates into sales transactions, you will struggle. Target was outperforming Walmart because their top-line was growing, while Walmart's revenue fell. When you analyze the total change in revenue from stores open at least a year and online sales, you get a more telling picture of how Target was outperforming Walmart. Target's same-store growth was 2.3% versus Walmart's 1.1% while the Target's online revenue growth was 38% versus Walmart's 17%.

In May 2015, the ultimate measure of Target's improved performance over Walmart is the way in which Target was extracting profitability from its operations. According to the S&P report, Target's improved profit performance lay in driving revenue up faster than costs; in contrast, that fundamental formula for success was seen as out of balance at Walmart.

WHAT A DIFFERENCE A YEAR MAKES

Fast forward to May 2016 with two of the business news headlines reading, "Walmart surges 9.6% on sales lift" and "Target shares plunge as sales fall, outlook spooks Street."

The driver for this success at Walmart is higher-than-expected quarterly profit as sales in their U.S. market rose, sending the retailer's shares up nearly 10 percent. Walmart was not only exceeding Wall Street's expectations; they have set themselves apart as one of the few retail success stories in 2016 as the rest of the industry struggles with how to adjust to the severe volatility in consumer spending.

The problem for Target is they missed analysts' estimates on first-quarter sales while reporting that second quarter sales will be flat to down 2% as shoppers pull back their spending making it harder to complete a sales transaction. The CEO of Target, Brian Cornell reported that "we continue to see consumers spend cautiously ...it's been a very wet and cold start to the year in the Northeast, and it's been reflected in our sales" on his call with the media.

While the Target CEO cited weather issues as a factor driving lower sales, I like how Walmart credited its higher sales to efforts made to provide shoppers with a better experience. The reason stated for Walmart's success while other retailers struggle is better pricing, selection, and fully stocked grocery shelves. In 2015, Walmart had identified these as areas they needed to improve, particularly for their smaller-format Neighborhood Market stores that had same-store sales increase of 7.1% in the quarter.

The U.S. CEO of Walmart, Greg Foran on his call with media said, "Investment in wages, training and store improvements are beginning to pay off." Walmart's success validates just as discussed in Chapter 7 relating to the 5th Organizing Principle involving your people and "why," that improvements in customer service make it easier for customers to find and buy what they want. In May 2016, Investors reacted to Walmart's sales growth by sending Walmart shares up $6.05 a share to close at $69.20 while Target's shares closed down 7.6% to $68.00 because of declining sales.

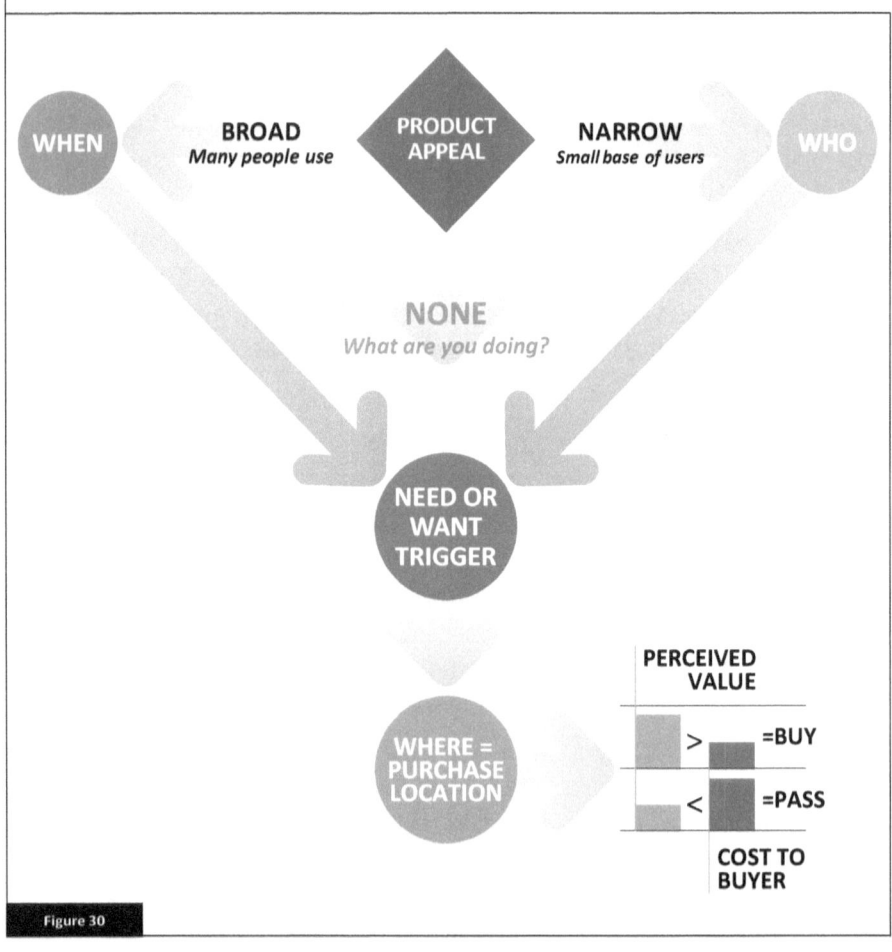

Figure 30

THE 7-P FRAMEWORK WORKS

I decided to discuss these two retail giants in the conclusion to Owning a GREAT Business because all of us have shopped at a Walmart and a Target at least once in our lives. We can relate to these businesses because we have been their customers, so it's a fitting business performance comparison. You may even have a preference for one store over another. My personal preference is not to shop at either retailer, whereas my brother works at Walmart, and my youngest daughter enjoys walking the aisles of Target.

What is your trigger as a customer about these two large stores? What are they doing right? What are they doing wrong, in your estimation? What would you do differently?

As you reflect on the many "decision tree" figures used throughout this book, I hope you find them helpful. Incorporate them in your planning as you think through the seven organizing principles for owning a great business.

What are they doing right? What are they doing wrong, in your estimation? What would you do differently?

This last figure shown on the previous page reinforces that whether your product appeal involves a narrow or broad customer base nothing good happens for your business unless a need or want trigger is activated for your customer. Once they make the decision to buy the next decision is where to make the purchase. Here is where they will make the final perceived value to cost determination.

In 2015, the perceived value was with Target yet in 2016 it shifted to Walmart. This reversal of results confirms the importance of knowing what your customers' value in the products your business produces and the services your business provides.

Target made changes to their product mix in 2015 that "shifted its focus to signature-product categories," such as apparel, and home and beauty. This move allowed them to charge premium prices, which boosted their gross profit margin (the profit left after paying direct costs, such as the cost of the product.) This business strategy worked in 2015 as people saw value in these upgraded products, they were prepared to pay a premium price. They could purchase these superior products at Target, but not at Walmart.

Yet in 2016, Walmart was reporting the better results because of adjustments they made to their pricing strategy while making investments in wages, training, and store improvements resulted in them starting off 2016 better than their direct competitors.

CONCLUSION:

OWNING A GREAT BUSINESS IS WITHIN YOUR REACH

Owning a great business is within your reach, if you really want it. You must want to start or enhance a business or you would not have been drawn to this book.

Owning a great business begins with mastering the seven organizing principles and applying the 7-P Framework to your unique business dynamics. As you apply these organizing principles to:

- Who you serve, you define your target customer
- What problems you solve, you confirm your products and services
- When your customers need your help, tells you their purchase trigger
- Where your customers will want you to help them, identifies your place
- Why it should matter to your employees and
- How you are better than your competitors, is how you develop the clarity and precision in your own business to ensure that your business earns a profit.

LEARN FROM EXPERTS

Successful crime show writers already know what we need to know if we are to avoid any of the seven fatal flaws in business. Every successful crime show has, on average, a fifty-five-page script, covering the 5 W's + H in their storyline. Never is one of these elements missing. If the writers skipped over one of the fundamental building blocks to good storytelling, it would be an incomplete story. The 5 W's + H represent the "organizing principles" to be followed in writing a good story.

There is a lot of thought, planning and plain hard work involved in business, and many of us operate without much of a safety net. By looking hard at your business and seeing the big picture, you'll be able to identify the principles most important to your business. The good news for us hardworking business leaders, who want to own a great business, is that we don't have to spend equal time on each of the seven organizing principles.

You'll have to think through each of the 7-Ps on your way to identifying your most important principle(s). This is key, because these are the principles, which represent your greatest chance of success, as well as your greatest risk of failure. Failing to determine the answers to the crucial 7-P questions is not a viable option. Success in business is within your reach. You will build a long lasting company that will serve customers, employees, loved ones and community for many long years.

FINAL THOUGHTS

Thank you for being an entrepreneur. Thank you for buying this book and being a part of the economy that keeps your nation running. Remember, nothing happens in life until a sale is made. My favorite paragraph from this book, found in the middle of page 18.

"Once you know who your customer is, what problem they are trying to solve, when they are most likely to need your help, and where they will want to transact business, you can define why and how they should value what you are offering, at a profitable price point. While this concept may seem simple on the surface, it amazes me how many business leaders fail to grasp these business fundamentals clearly, and apply them to the small to large decisions they make every day."

Thank you, again, for investing your time to read my book. My hope is that you have found the thoughts, observations and encouragement offered helpful. My contact information is listed below. Feel free to share any stories on how this book has helped you or question you may have. I want to be on your success team.

With appreciation,

Lorin Young
Owner, Design Dynamics
1641 Kaiser Avenue
Irvine, CA 92614

949.870.3320

lyoung@designdynamics.com

PS: *If you enjoyed this book and found value, please leave an honest review on Amazon or GoodReads. As in any business, the best advertising is word of mouth from satisfied customers.*

"My advice is don't keep asking yourself if you can do something.

Just get out there and do it.

You can really surprise yourself."

ROZ SAVAGE
TRANSOCEANIC OPEN WATER ROWER

APPENDIX

APPENDIX:
CONFIRMING WHAT I NEED TO DO DIFFERENTLY EXERCISE

In validating the seven organizing principles for owning a great business, I asked business leaders to share what they think causes businesses to fail. My goal in this research was to make sure I wasn't missing any potential pitfalls. I rarely walked away feeling upbeat; I can tell you that. But it was important to subject myself to this depressing line of thinking to confirm the 7-P Framework also identified what not do to.

Another challenge this research created was a serious bout of self-reflection. Discussing and researching what others have written about business failure caused me to think very clearly about what we are doing well, and where we can do better, in my own business. This is why I turned this research into an exercise for you to pause and reflect on how your own business is faring against known problem areas.

Owning a small business is a tough job that never ends. You can always be doing more, and yet you are already investing so much time, money, energy and heart in building your business. This is why choosing to focus on the critical few things you need to do, over the relevant many things you could do, is so important. The challenge is in knowing what is most important. Discovering the principles composed of concentrated truth for your business, packaged for application to a wide variety of circumstances, is how you get there.

Remember, that SmallBizTrends.com has confirmed that on average 40% of small businesses make a profit, 30% come out even, and the remaining 30% lose money. As a result, half of all businesses fail in less than five years. Protect yours from being one of the failures by completing the following exercise that begins with reading each item below carefully. Choose the most appropriate response from the response key relative to how true that statement is about your business. Remember, owning a great business is a gradual process, and no one is perfect. Your goal is to be honest with yourself and accept that you will rate yourself better on some items than on others.

Response Key:

1 =	Don't Experience	Not an Issue	Doing well	No Risk
2 =	Sometimes	Becoming an issue	Under control	Working out of
3 =	Often	Starting to improve	Could be better	Dealing with
4 =	Almost Always	Personal priority	Losing control	Concerned
5 =	Always	Need outside help	Out of control	Experiencing

1ˢᵀ Organizing Principle: WHO? (Target Customer)
NOT KNOWING PRECISELY WHO SHOULD BUY WHAT YOU HAVE TO OFFER.

- ☐ *Failure to identify, and then find, your target customer.* Results in you wasting your promotional investments because you don't have any target to focus your marketing campaigns on.
- ☐ *Unable to understand your customers' needs.* Guesswork leads to inefficient operations, marketing, and sales as you struggle to produce and sell unwanted products and services.
- ☐ *Not acting on customer feedback about what you could do better.* Keeps you doing what you have been doing while your customers take their business to someone who is acting on their feedback.
- ☐ *Too small of a customer base.* Too much of your revenue success is concentrated in one anchor client, resulting in your success being 100% dependent on their success.

2ⁿᵈ Organizing Principle: WHAT? (Product)
NOT KNOWING WHAT PROBLEM YOUR TARGET CUSTOMER IS TRYING TO SOLVE WITH THEIR PURCHASE FROM YOU.

- ☐ *Trying to be all things to all people to acquire top-line revenue.* This potential "fatal flaw" distracts you from investing the time and resources necessary to understand completely who buys your product and more importantly, why.
- ☐ *Falsely assuming that there is a market for the product or service you are offering.* You will not be successful in building a business in an industry where consumers don't see value in the products and services you offer, or in a market which is already declining, due to technological advances and other factors.
- ☐ *Not being able to deliver product when it is needed.* When people make the decision to buy, the decision is made, and they expect their product to be delivered at that moment. The have it now mentality that exists in our society means you need to either maintain sufficient inventory to meet demand or be able to create the product in the buying moment, or people will either go someplace else or do without.
- ☐ *Not enough product breadth. All your eggs in one basket with just one product or service.* This leads business owners to cling tightly to this one effort because it brings in good revenue. But when that one thing becomes less desirable and less able to compete in a large marketplace, their business goes on life support because they don't have a buffer against the endless ebb and flow of business tides.
- ☐ *Not enough product demand.* Highly specialized products that are expensive to produce in service to a narrow market need are at most risk for not being able to hold a price that a company can make a profit on, particularly when the people buying it have substitution options.

- **High product return rate.** All the marketing money in the world or talented sales and customer service professionals won't help a "crappy" product. You have to deliver a product that serves a need or satisfies a customer at a price that is viewed fair by your customer that results in profit for you.

3rd Organizing Principle: WHEN? (Place1)
NOT KNOWING WHEN YOUR TARGET WILL NEED OR WANT YOUR PRODUCTS OR SERVICES.

- **Unable to generate leads.** Marketing measures indicating your marketing is being seen, but you aren't getting leads indicates you either have a timing, messaging, call to action, or a product problem. Either way, you are spending money that isn't producing a return for your business. Keep it up and you won't have any money left to fund your operations.
- **Too reliant on customer created demand.** Means that demand creation for your products and services occurs outside of your control with your customers. This works as long as they keep buying. When the orders drop off, then it's up to your marketing skills to create demand for what you to.
- **Uneven or unexplained cyclicality.** Every business develops a rhythm to it and when that semi-predictable flow of sales becomes unpredictable your business is at high risk for failing if you are unable to adjust your overhead expenses simultaneously with your drops in sales.
- **People stop buying all of a sudden.** Changes in technology, declining consumer demand, or increasing competition from huge companies with more buying power and advertising dollars.

4th Organizing Principle: WHERE? (Place2)
NOT KNOWING WHERE THEY WILL WANT TO MAKE THE PURCHASE.

- **Wrong location:** If your business has a "bricks and mortar" location, you need to make sure that you are convenient to your customers, and near to your suppliers and your employees.
- **People can't find my website:** Your odds of people stumbling across your website are extremely low. The digital marketing world is becoming increasingly fragmented and expensive to work with. If you don't have the expertise to do it yourself or budget to buy from someone who does your online business is in grave risk.
- **Poor choice of location:** Never let a cheap lease tempt you into choosing the wrong location. Consider your competition (how many similar businesses are located nearby?) and your accessibility (is the area well served by freeways, public transportation, and foot traffic?). Even something as simple as traffic patterns and parking can make or break your business success; often it is the little things that make a big difference

5th Organizing Principle: WHY? (People)
YOUR EMPLOYEES DO NOT KNOW THE WHY BEHIND WHAT THEY DO WHEN THEY PROVIDE SERVICE TO YOUR CUSTOMERS.

- ☐ **Poor execution:** Poor customer service and overall employee incompetence will quickly sink your business. Make sure your employees place a premium on customer service. Develop systems and processes for how tasks should be accomplished, model appropriate customer interactions, and create internal controls to monitor compliance.

- ☐ **Miserable employees.** You can easily spot this by an employee's willingness to SMILE at a customer, their willingness to go the extra mile to make things right, or even their willingness to say, "I'm sorry," (show compassion) when a mistake occurs. Poor employee moral (even the presence of one angry, unhappy, or depressed employee) will cause major havoc, quickly.

- ☐ **Poor customer service.** Guaranteed to occur 100% of the time any customer interaction is considered an inconvenience. Protect for this by watching how customers get their questions answered, whether phone calls and emails are returned promptly, accurate billing is provided, win-win problem solving occurs without you, and there is an overall, pleasant demeanor in your employees.

- ☐ **Getting complacent:** Accepting the status quo, mediocrity, or stagnation results in a lack of attention to what the customer wants, and how these wants are changing over time.

- ☐ **Employees** who don't see the noble purpose in what they do. Until your employees see the value in what they do, they will not go the extra mile nor give their discretionary effort to produce extraordinary results. The best you can hope for is they will do their job.

- ☐ **Holding onto employees that you know should be let go.** When you have an employee who isn't a good fit for your culture you do them, your customers, and their coworkers a disservice by keeping them on your team. While it's never easy to fire someone, sometimes it's the best thing for the employee. In the long-term they are likely to thank you while in the short-term their coworkers will celebrate your finally taking action.

6th Organizing Principle: HOW? (Promotion + Packaging)
FAILING TO ARTICULATE HOW THE BUYER WILL BENEFIT:

- ☐ **Weak value proposition:** Few, if any, customers can articulate why they chose to buy from your over someone else. And if they can't articulate this, they will not be bringing more customers to your business.

- ☐ **Ineffective marketing:** Customers can't do business with you if they don't know you exist. It doesn't cost a lot to advertise and promote your business through online marketing, social media, email, local search, and more. But these costs do need to be factored into your business plan.

- **Ineffective sales techniques:** Once you have a potential customer, you have to know how to lead them down the sales path (remember the funnel?) To the endpoint: buying the things they need or want. Too many people see sales as a dirty part of the business when it can be one of the most satisfying aspects. The key is learning to see the sales process as helping people buy the things they need. Or, in a different type of business, providing the customer with information or other services.
- **Underestimating the competition:** Customer loyalty doesn't just happen—you have to earn it. Watch your competition closely, and stay one step ahead of them. If you don't take care of your customers, your competition certainly will. Customers will go where they can find the best products and services. It's important for you to know who your competition is, what they have to offer, and what makes your products or services better.
- **The stronger the demand for a product or service, the greater the supply.** When supply is high, you must have a strong value proposition to stand out from your competitors. And remember that any competitors who offer similar products and services, at a lower price, provide greater value than you do.
- **Inadequate sales or overly optimistic revenue plans.** Not having the flexibility to adjust when revenue is less than planned or it takes longer than planned to begin coming in. This is especially important for new businesses.

7th Organizing Principle: PROFITS! (Price)
NONE OF THE 5 W'S + H MATTERS IF YOU DON'T MAKE A PROFIT.

- **Pricing yourself out of the market.** One of the most common challenges for those operating with a product innovative or customer intimate strategic style against an operationally excellent competitor who has what they need.
- **Price disadvantage.** The business is competing on price against a national competitor's economies of scale.
- **Poor cash flow.** This dynamic causes you to run out of cash due to inadequate sales, faulty budgeting, or poor planning.
- **Poor accounting practices.** Poor record keeping and financial controls, i.e., poor accounting for money coming in and going out put a business on a path straight toward failure. If you don't know what is going on financially, you do not have good control of your business. With bad numbers or no numbers, your business is flying blind.
- **Operational inefficiencies.** Paying too much for rent, labor, and materials will leave your company uncompetitive, unprofitable, and ultimately at a sales disadvantage to those who are operationally efficient.

- ☐ **Over-investment in fixed assets and overhead.** Causes you to financially overextend your business. As in "under-capitalized with insufficient cash reserves," this creates the same challenge of doing business on a tightrope, in high winds, without a safety net
- ☐ **Over-expansion.** This can be the result of moving into markets that are not as profitable, experiencing growing pains that damage the business, or borrowing too much money in an attempt to keep growth at a particular rate.
- ☐ **Under-capitalized.** Insufficient cash reserves rob you of a working "capital cushion" for unforeseen events and is like operating your business without a safety net. The good news is that you can. The bad news is that you have little-to-no margin for error, between making a mistake—which can happen to anyone—and going out of business.
- ☐ **Financial mismanagement** from not knowing where the money in your business is coming from (revenue), or where the money is going (costs) can arise due to lack of skill or interest in managing cash flow, taxes, expenses, and other financial issues.

General business management/ownership challenges

- ☐ **Inadequate business plan.** A well thought-out business plan forces you to think about the future and the challenges you will face. It forces you to consider your financial needs, your marketing and management plans, your competition, and your overall strategy. You know you have a viable business plan when it helps you to focus on your goals and your vision and lays out a clear plan to realize them.
- ☐ **Dysfunctional leadership in your business.** This dynamic affects every aspect of your operation, from financial management to employee morale; once your productivity begins to suffer, your ability to manage operational costs is lost.
- ☐ **Inability or unwillingness to adapt.** Failing to adapt to a changing market, resulting from changes in consumer tastes and buying habits, will result in a loss of customers and ultimately the loss of your business.
- ☐ **Failing to change with the times:** Related to the above, the ability to recognize opportunities and be flexible enough to adapt is crucial to surviving and thriving. As a business owner, it's important to learn to wear multiple hats, respond nimbly, and develop new areas of expertise.

Now go back through the list and highlight any items you gave a four or a five rating to. If you have none, congratulations you are running an impressive company. If you have multiple, identify which organizing principle has more 5s and 4s vs. 1s and 2s and you have identified your most critical organizing principle to master.

If you found this exercise helpful, then I invite you to look at page 132 to see our announcement for the *Owning a GREAT Business Roadmap* a companion guide to greater success with this book. This new book will help you develop your answers to areas of concern you just identified above through a series of self-guided exercises by organizing principle. As you complete each exercise, you will accelerate your application of the seven organizing principles to your unique business dynamics you need to realize higher revenues and profits.

DON'T LET THIS HAPPEN TO YOUR BUSINESS.

Apply the principles from the 7-P Framework to help you realize better results for your business.

ABOUT THE AUTHOR

LORIN YOUNG

Lorin Young began his career in the retail grocery industry with Stater Bros Markets, where he mastered the ability to provide exceptional customer service. Following graduate school, Lorin joined industry leader Pittsburgh Plate Glass, where he successfully opened the commercial market for the high-performance "Environ" coil coating product line. The key account and product management experience gained during his tenure with PPG served him well when he later moved into the financial services industry, first with Nationwide Insurance and subsequently with Veterinary Pet Insurance.

Throughout his career, in positions as diverse as Marketing, Sales, Corporate Communications, Human Resources, Strategic Planning and Operations, Lorin has been commended for his ability to assess talent, determine organizational deficits and prioritize customer needs. His ability to see "the big picture" has enabled Lorin to develop initiatives that turned around struggling enterprises and enabled growing businesses to blossom.

Today, Lorin is the founder of Keystone Revenue Solutions, Inc., and owner of Design Dynamics, a wide-format digital printer and signage company located in Irvine, California. He loves owning a great business and has now translated his experience and knowledge into helping other entrepreneurs achieve their professional goals.

Lorin's MBA from Brigham Young University and his BA in Marketing Management, from California State University, Fullerton, coupled with more than twenty-five years of success in key leadership roles qualify him to astutely address the challenges of today's business leaders and tomorrow's entrepreneurs.

LORIN YOUNG SPEAKS TO THE FOLLOWING TOPICS, INCLUDING:

Owning a GREAT Business
7 Organizing Principles So Yours Is One of Them

The Keystone to Revenue Success
Profitability, Plus Sales Growth

Being a GREAT Place to Do Business BEGINS with Being a GREAT Place to Work
Integrating the 6 Ps with the 6 B's for the Keystone to Profitability

You Can't Lead if You Don't Manage Through Metric
You Can't Act On What You Don't Measure

Overcoming Fear
Making the Leap from Fortune 100 Executive to Small Business Owner

Being a Corporate Leader vs. Running Your Own Business
What it Takes, Lessons Learned, and Advice

Why Marketing Fails and What You Can Do to Fix It
Marketing Is More Than Advertising; It's Decision Science

You can reach Lorin Young for speaking engagements or other opportunities, at: lorin@lorinyoung.com, or call him at 949.870.3320.

WHAT'S NEXT?
Having Read *Owning a GREAT Businesss*, You may be wrestling with "How do I apply these Principles?"

The *Owning a GREAT Business Roadmap* has been designed by Lorin Young as a companion guidebook to this book. The additional resource will help you develop your answers to questions you are wrestling with right now. He has created a series of self-guided exercises by organizing principle to help you accelerate your application of the seven organizing principles to your unique business dynamics.

Owning a great business is within your reach when you know, with clarity, who your customer is, what problem they are trying to solve, when are they most likely to need your help, and where will they want to buy from you! Knowing the theory to these key principles can be hard to build on until you start making better decisions with confidence. The *Owning a GREAT Business Roadmap* will help you identify then initiate improvement plans with confidence. As you complete each exercise, your confidence will increase as you deepen your learning and broaden your perspective. You will develop new insights and effective action plans to execute so you too, will own a great business.

To learn more about this valuable tool, go to **www.owningagreatbusiness.com**. Never before has such an array of strategy exercises, mental frameworks and tactical decision guides been assembled in one book. Move beyond the theory. Use the roadmap to help you navigate the important decisions you need to enhance your ability to profit from the insights you are developing through the 7-P Framework.

SOURCE CITATION PLUS FIGURE & TABLE GUIDE BY CHAPTER

Preface
Thomas Monson quote, 3
- "In Quest of the Abundant Life." Thomas S. Monson – Ensign – March 1988

Introduction
Producing a Winning Business Formula

Johann Wolfgang von Goethe quote, 4
- retrieved from BrainyQuote.com website: http://www.brainyquote.com/quotes/quotes/j/johannwolf150574.html

Top 10 Crime Dramas from the 1990's images, 6

Law & Order (NBC, 1990 - 2010)

Matlock (NBC/ABC, 1986 - 1995)

JAG (NBC/CBS, 1995 - 2005)

Nash Bridges (CBS, 1996 - 2001)

Diagnosis Murder (CBS, 1983 – 2001)

Homicide: Life on the Street (NBC, 1993 - 1999)

THE X-FILES (FOX, 1993 - 2002)

Murder She Wrote (CBS, 1984 - 1996)

N.Y.P.D. Blue (ABC 1993 - 2005)

Walker, Texas Ranger (CBS, 1993 - 2001)

TV script statistics from "Crafty TV writing: thinking inside the box." Alex Epstein, 6
- Owl Books – 2006

Chapter 1
The Difficulties of Owning a GREAT Business

Vernon Law quote, 9
- retrieved from BrainyQuote.com website: http://www.brainyquote.com/quotes/quotes/v/vernonlaw115255.html

U.S. Government study "Why Customers Stop Buying" referenced by David Bater "5 Reasons Why Customers Stop Buying AND How to Make Sure it Doesn't Happen to You!" posted May 14, 2012
- retrieved from DavidBater.com website: http://davidbater.com/why-customers-stop-buying/

Figure 1: Decisions getting made in the dark leads to losses, 12

Figure 2: Number of decisions small business owners must deal with, 13

Vernon Law quote, 15
- retrieved from BrainyQuote.com website: http://www.brainyquote.com/quotes/quotes/v/vernonlaw115256.html

Chapter 2
7 Organizing Principles for Owning a Great Business

William Bruce Cameron Quote, 16
- "Informal Sociology: A Casual Introduction to Sociological Thinking" - William Bruce Cameron - Random House - 1963

Psychology Today, quote from Ryon Howes, 19
- retrieved from PsychologyToday.com website: https://www.psychologytoday.com/blog/in-therapy/200907/the-definition-insanity-is

"Fundamental Principles of Physics" - F. Woodbridge Constant, 20 s- Addison-Wesley Pub. – 1967 and "Fundamental Laws of Physics" - F. Woodbridge Constant - Addison-Wesley - 1963

Figure 3: The 7-P Framework, 22

Figure 4: The importance of people in the exchange of value that serves a need or satisfies a want, 23

Figure 5: The exchange of value will result in a Buy or Pass and a Profit or Loss, 24

Figure 6: The impact on business when it's a Pass or Loss, 24

Figure 7: Reinforces the importance of the exchange of value to your success, 25

Figure 8: The transactional enablers of When, Where and How, 26

Chapter 3
1ST Organizing Principle: WHO? (Target Customer)

Arthur Schopenhauer quote, 30
- retrieved from BrainyQuote.com website: http://www.brainyquote.com/quotes/quotes/a/arthurscho385253.html

Figure 9: Product appeal is either broad, narrow or none, 32

Law & Order (NBC, 1990 - 2010), 35

Chapter 4
2nd Organizing Principle: WHAT? (Product)

Peter Drucker quote, 36
- retrieved from BrainyQuote.com website: http://www.brainyquote.com/quotes/quotes/p/peterdruck154444.html

Figure 10: Options when your product appeal is unproven vs proven, 39

Darwin quote in question, 41
- retrieved from QuoteInvestigator.com website: http://quoteinvestigator.com/2014/05/04/adapt/

Keurig facts, 43-44
- retrieved from Money.CNN.com: http://money.cnn.com/2015/05/06/investing/keurig-green-mountain-earnings-stock-fall/

JAG (NBC/CBS, 1995 - 2005), 44-45

Abraham Lincoln quote, 45
- retrieved from goodreads.com website: http://www.goodreads.com/quotes/328848-the-best-way-to-predict-your-future-is-to-create

Chapter 5
3rd Organizing Principle: WHEN? (Place1)

Yogi Berra quote, 46
- retrieved from BrainyQuote.com website: http://www.brainyquote.com/quotes/quotes/y/yogiberra621249.html

Figure 11: What makes people buy comparison between needs and wants, 49

Figure 12: Consumer to customer progression model, 51

"SPIN Selling" - Neil Rackham, 51-52
- McGraw-Hill – 1988

Figure 13: Benefits to costs scale, 52

Murder She Wrote (CBS, 1984 - 1996), 54

Chapter 6
4th Organizing Principle: WHERE? (Place2)

Buzz Aldrin quote, 57 - retrieved from BrainyQuote.com website: http://www.brainyquote.com/quotes/quotes/b/buzzaldrin679850.html

Figure 14: Place comes down to knowing or not knowing your location, 58

Hostess Brands facts, 58-59
- retrieved from USAToday.com website: http://americasmarkets.usatoday.com/2015/03/25/hostess-pulled-a-zinger/

Figure 15: Is your business driven by your physical or online location, 59

Figure 16: Is your buyer mode transactional or relational in dealing with you, 61

Table 1: Design Dynamics customer buying preferences tiers, 62

Figure 17: Value triangle of quality, speed and price, 63

Table 2: Design Dynamics good, better, best by the value triangle, 64

Table 3: Design Dynamics degree of difficult by process step, 65

Murder She Wrote (CBS, 1984 - 1996), 66

Buzz Aldrin quote, 67
- retrieved from BrainyQuote.com website: http://www.brainyquote.com/quotes/quotes/b/buzzaldrin679870.html

Chapter 7
5th Organizing Principle: WHY? (People)

Warren Bennis quote, 68
- retrieved from BrainyQuote.com website: http://www.brainyquote.com/quotes/quotes/w/warrenbenn120865.html

"Discipline of Market Leaders" - Michael Treacy - Frederik D. Wiersema, 70
- Addison-Wesley Pub. Co. - 1995

Figure 18: Visual for operational excellence, product leadership and customer intimacy, 70

"The Talent Solution: aligning strategy and people to achieve extraordinary results" - Edward L.Gubman, 72-73
- McGraw-Hill - 1998

Table 4: "The Talent Solution" concepts aligned to "The Discipline of Market Leaders," 73

Jack Parsons, 74-75

Former VPI and PurinaCare Executive, 75-77

Law & Order (NBC, 1990 - 2010), 78

Warren Bennis quote, 79
- retrieved from BrainyQuote.com website:
 http://www.brainyquote.com/quotes/quotes/w/warrenbenn121190.html

Chapter 8
6th Organizing Principle: HOW? (Promotion + Packaging)

P. T. Barnum quote, 80
- retrieved from BrainyQuote.com website: http://www.brainyquote.com/quotes/quotes/p/ptbarnum539959.html

Figure 19: Breaking through the noise to earn a purchase transaction, 82

Table 5: Four keys to effective promotional messaging, 83

Figure 20: Keys to effective promotion when unaware vs aware, 84

Figure 21: Awareness to love progression funnel, 85

Figure 22: Demonstrating the importance of promotion with the remaining 6 Ps of marketing via your hand, 86

Table 6: Common promotional elements by marketing mix element, 87

Matlock (NBC/ABC, 1986 - 1995), 88

P. T. Barnum quote, 89
- retrieved from BrainyQuote.com website: http://www.brainyquote.com/quotes/quotes/p/ptbarnum539973.html ....

Chapter 9
7th Organizing Principle: PROFITS! (Price)

John Glenn quote, 90
- retrieved from Goodreads.com website: http://www.goodreads.com/quotes/959148-as-i-hurtled-through-space-one-thought-kept-crossing-my

Figure 23: Options when your price is lower or higher, 92

Figure 24: Price/Value formula showing good and bad value, 93

"Selections from the Wealth of Nations" - Adam Smith, 94-95
- Appleton-Century-Crofts – 1957

Figure 25: Visual representation of the effect on price when supply or demand changes, 95

Disneyland tickets to cost as much as $119 on peak days, as park turns to demand based pricing, 96-97
- retrieved from OCRegister.com website: http://www.ocregister.com/-articles/disney-706040-pricing-days.html

Nash Bridges (CBS, 1996 - 2001), 97-98

John Glenn quote, 99
- retrieved from forbes.com quotes website: http://www.forbes.com/quotes/5263/

Chapter 10
One More Nugget or Three of Wisdom ...

John Wanamaker quote, 100
- retrieved from QuotationsPage.com website: http://www.quotationspage.com/quote/1992.html

"Good to Great: why some companies make the leap and others don't" - James C.Collins, 101
- HarperBusiness - 2001

Figure 26: The three fundamental growth strategies, 104

Figure 27: Customers already buying from you equal a straight line transaction connection, 105

Tricia Duryee of Geek Wire post, 106
- retrieved from GeekWire.com website: http://www.geekwire.com/2015/amazons-40-million-prime-members-spending-1500-year-average/

RMS Titanic facts, 107-110
- sourced from Wikipedia.org website: https://en.wikipedia.org/wiki/RMS_Titanic

Figure 28: Whether product appeal is broad or narrow you still need a trigger, 113

Figure 29: Challenge of breaking through the noise when your business is unknown, 114

"Why Target is reviving faster than Walmart," 115
- retrieved from USAToday.com website: http://americasmarkets.usatoday.com/2015/05/20/why-target-is-reviving-faster-than-walmart/

"Walmart surges 9.6% on sales lift," 115-116
- retrieved from USAToday.com website:
http://www.usatoday.com/story/money/2016/05/19/walmart-first-quarter-earnings/84551226/ and "Target shares plunge as sales fall, outlook spooks Street"
http://www.usatoday.com/story/money/2016/05/18/target-first-quarter-earnings/84530886/

Figure 30: Once the need or want is triggered it comes down to where and perceived value, 116

Conclusion
Owning a GREAT business is within your reach

Tin Cup movie quote, 118
- retrieved from IMDb.com website: http://www.imdb.com/title/tt0117918/quotes

Roz Savage quote, 121
- retrieved from BrainyQuote.com website:
http://www.brainyquote.com/quotes/quotes/r/rozsavage554007.html

Appendix
Confriming What I Need to do Differently Excercise

SmallBizTrends.com stats, 123
- retrieved from SmallBizTrends.com website: http://smallbiztrends.com/2013/03/infographic-failed-small-businesses.html

About the Author
None

INDEX

A
Accounting
Cash flow protection, 24–25, 29
Cash gone → Business gone, 11, 15, 24–25, 27, 91
Counting vs. things that count, 16
Fundamentals of business, 12–13
Opportunity costs, 93–94
Percentage profitable small businesses, 123
Sales costs, 25–26, 27, 110
Half-wasted expense, 100, 110
Marketing budget, 86
Prospects vs. suspects, 110–112
Top-line importance, 115–117
Adaptability, 20
Advertising. See also marketing; promotion
Advertising campaigns, 83, 85–86
Definition, 83
Internet marketing, 60
Sales costs, 25–26, 27, 110
Half-wasted expense, 100, 110
Marketing budget, 86
Prospects vs. suspects, 110–112
Trigger to purchase, 113–114
Word of mouth best, 120
Ad Words (Google), 60
Affinity in purchase process, 52–53
Affordable Healthcare Act mandated purchase, 52
Aldrin, Buzz
On opportunities opening doors, 67
On right place, right time, 56
Amazon customer maximization, 106
Appeal of product, 32–33
Attracting new customers, 102–103, 104–106, 110

B
Barnum, P.T.
On promotion or nothing, 80
On thorough understanding of business, 89
Becker, Tom
Tires to NASCAR fans, 48
Believe in yourself
Framework commitment, 28–29, 119
Get out there and do it, 121
Great things are accomplished, 68
Investing in oneself, 1
Benchmarking, 42
Benefits not features
Price and value, 92, 93
Problem product solves, 81
What is the product, 38–39
Bennis, Warren
On environment to flourish, 79
On talent and belief, 68
Berra, Yogi
On timing over power, 46
Blockbuster Video and change, 41–42
Built to Last (Collins), 101

Business
1. Know: who, what, when, where for profitable price, 18, 120
5W's + H, 22, 28, 84. See also framework for success
Adjustments for big impact, 112–117
Attracting new customers, 102–103, 104–106, 110
Critical success factor, 55
Customer–management separation, 103
Definition, 12, 13, 91
Customer needs plus profit, 32
Difficulties of business
Buying stops, 11–12, 15, 87, 107. See also Buying
Cash, 11, 15. See also cash
Decision making, 12, 13–15. See also decision making
Employees who "fit," 72–73. See also employees
Failure
1. Buying stops, 11–12, 15, 87, 107
2. Cash gone, 11, 15, 24–25, 27, 91
Avoiding, 123–128
Credibility loss, 9
Customers not understood, 18, 31, 33
Percentage surviving, 11
Product complacency, 40–42
Violation of principles, 8, 88, 98, 119
Fundamentals of, 12–13
Good as enemy of great, 101–102
Growth strategies, 104–106. See also growth
Innovation, 38
Leadership establishing why, 74–77
Top-line importance, 115–117
Reflection for perspective, 19, 22, 123, 132
Roadmap companion guidebook, 132
Strategic style, 70–73
Target customer identification, 23–25, 28, 31–35, 45. See also customers
Tools for the job, 108–109
Top-line importance, 115–117
Uncontrollable factors, 109–110
Buying
Affinity, 52–53
Buying stops, 11–12, 15, 87, 107
Cost:Benefit ratio, 52
Experimentation mode, 51, 53
Motivation to buy
Price and purchasing decision, 51
Promotion goal, 86–87
Question for source of, 32
Want vs. need, 49, 50, 52
Process of, 50–53, 85, 112
Price and, 92–93, 94
Promotion and, 85, 86
Prospects vs. suspects, 110–112
Trigger to purchase, 113–114, 116
Transactional vs. relational, 61–66
Buzz word avoidance, 82

C

Cameron, William Bruce
On counting vs. things that count, 16
Capturing new customers, 102–103, 104–106, 110
Cash
Cash flow protection, 24–25, 29
Cash for sales costs, 25–26, 27, 110
Half-wasted expense, 100, 110
Marketing budget, 86
Prospects vs. suspects, 110–112
Cash gone → business gone, 11, 15, 24–25, 27, 91
Change
Adjustments for big impact, 112–117
Framework commitment, 28–29
Necessity of, 19, 41
Shoulda happened, 41, 59
Survival and, 41
Chicago (IL) and change, 59
Cincinnati (OH) and change, 59
Collins, Jim
Built to Last, 101
Good to Great, 101
Communication
Compelling graphics, 39
Message, 82
Customer care and, 109–110
Employee training in greatness, 9, 18, 22, 27, 28, 66
Asking why, 69–70, 71–73, 83, 87
Promotion, 83. See also promotion
Consistency, 87
Promotional mix, 84, 86–87
Prospects vs. suspects, 111–112
Unique selling proposition, 81–83
Companion guidebook Roadmap, 132
Company. See business
Connecting with customers, 7–8. See also customers; relationships
Consistent communication, 87
Constant, F. Woodbridge
Principles vs. laws, 20
Cornell, Brian (Target), 115–116
COST:BENEFIT ratio of buying, 52
Courage. See believe in yourself; fear of mistakes
Cousins Tackle niche marketing, 34
Credibility and jumping the shark, 9
Crime dramas. See TV crime dramas
Critical success factor, 55
Cross-selling, 105–106
Cuse, Carlton (Nash Bridges), 97
Customers
Broad vs. narrow base, 32–33, 34
Trigger to purchase, 113, 116
"When" and broad base, 55
Buying process, 50–53, 85, 112
Affinity, 52–53
Experimentation mode, 51, 53
Price and, 92–93, 94
Promotion and, 85, 86
Prospects vs. suspects, 110–112
Trigger to purchase, 113–114, 116
Buying stops, 11–12, 15, 87, 107
Caring about, 11–12, 87, 107, 108
Uncontrollable factors, 109–110
Communication consistency, 87
Creating value for, 27–28
Critical success factor, 55
Customer intimacy strategy, 70–73
"Doing it themselves," 94
Failure to understand, 18, 31, 33
Knowledge is king, 44–45, 105–106
Listening to
Leadership in great businesses, 75
Product development, 40, 42, 43–44
Prospects vs. suspects, 111–112
Management separation from, 103
Needs to be met, 18, 20, 25, 26, 28, 103–104
Profit versus, 106
Wants vs. needs, 47–48, 49, 50–51, 52
New customers, 102–103, 104–106, 110
Problem for product to solve, 37–39, 44–45
Product relationship, 32–33, 36
Promotion relevancy importance, 84, 86–87
Prospects vs. suspects, 110–112
Questions to ask, 32
Retained customers, 50–54
Disney theme parks, 97
Loss of, 102, 104–106, 107
Maximization of, 105, 107
Service experience
Customer needs and business scope, 103–104
Employee disconnect, 70, 87
Physical location vs. online, 60, 62, 63
Transactional vs. relational purchase, 61–66
Suspects vs. prospects, 110–112
"Sweet spot" of pricing, 24–25, 29
Target customer identification, 23–25, 28, 31–35, 45
Exercise to avoid business failure, 124
As key, 23–24, 35, 36
Prospects vs. suspects, 110–112
Questions to ask, 32
Trigger to purchase, 113–114
Where purchases occur, 58, 59–60
Transactional vs. relational purchase, 61–66

D

Darwin, Charles
On change and survival, 41
Decision making
Blindly, 12
Customer purchase decisions, 51–53, 85, 92–93, 112
Delegating, 72, 74
Employees as problem solvers, 72, 73, 104, 107
Fear of mistakes, 2, 92–93
Information gathering, 5–6, 17, 69
Poor decision not fatal, 8
Process of, 15, 22, 74, 132
Roadmap companion guidebook, 132
Small business vs. large, 2, 13, 14, 15
Step back for perspective, 19, 22, 123, 132
Demand and supply, 94–95, 96–97
Demand-driven pricing model, 96–97

Design Dynamics
Broad customer base, 55
Customer care and loss, 109–110
Online marketing, 60
Owner Lorin Young, 1, 2, 13, 14, 103, 131
Supply and demand, 95
Target customer, 34
Transactional vs. relational purchases, 61–66
Diagnosis Murder (TV show), 6, 134
Discipline of Market Leaders (Treacy & Wiersema), 70
Disneyland pricing, 96–97
Drucker, Peter
On knowing customer, 36
Duryee, Tricia (Geek Wire), 106

E
Employees
Communication to customers, 87
Dependent on business, 1, 29
Purchase–paycheck disconnect, 69–70
Employees who "fit," 72–73
Empowering to serve, 72, 104, 107, 108
"Face" of business, 23, 66
Ownership in company culture, 70, 78, 83
As problem solvers, 72, 73, 104, 107
Sales lost by, 11, 66, 70, 87, 107
Small business vs. large, 13, 14
Training in greatness, 9, 18, 22, 27, 28, 66
Asking why, 69–70, 71–73, 78, 83, 87, 116
Price/value equation, 93
Tools for the job, 108–109
Walmart success, 116
Value adding by, 38, 60, 66, 70
Executive summaries
1. Know: who, what, when, where for profitable price, 18, 120
Avoiding business failure, 123–128
Business without profit, 98
Customer knowledge, 44, 45
Framework for success, 22–29
Repeat customers, 50
Transactional vs. relational purchase, 62, 64, 65
"Why" employees and values, 78
Exercises for reflection
Avoiding business failure, 123–128
Roadmap companion guidebook, 132
Experimentation mode of buying, 51, 53

F
Factors outside your control, 109–110
Failure of businesses
1. Buying stops, 11–12, 15, 87, 107
2. Cash gone, 11, 15, 24–25, 27, 91
Avoiding, 123–128
Credibility loss, 9
Customers not understood, 18, 31, 33
Percentage surviving, 11
Product complacency, 40–42
Violation of principles, 8, 88, 98, 119
Fear of mistakes
Customer purchase decision, 92–93
Decision paralysis, 2
Face troubles with courage, 3

Poor decision not fatal, 8
Financial information management system (FIMS), 103
Fischer, Peter S. (Murder She Wrote), 66
Fleet, Frederick (Titanic), 108, 109
Follower or innovator, 43–44
Food buying variety, 27
Foran, Greg (Walmart), 116
4 P's of marketing, 17, 37, 91
Framework for success
1. Who is the customer. See also customers
About this step, 23–25, 28
Broad vs. narrow base, 32–33, 34, 55, 113, 116
Target customer as key, 35, 36
Target customer exercise, 124
Target customer identification, 23–25, 28, 31–35
Target customer questions to ask, 32
Target customer "where," 58, 59–60
2. What is the product
About this step, 25–26, 28
Benefits not features, 38–39
Broad or narrow customer base, 32–33, 34, 55, 113, 116
Buying process, 50–53, 85, 112. See also buying
Exercise to avoid business failure, 124
Follower vs. innovator, 43
Growth strategies, 105–106
New vs. existing, 38, 39–40
Packaging, 25, 39, 40, 87
Place, 40. See also place
Price, 40. See also price
Problem–solution, 37–39, 48–49
Product development, 40–42, 50, 97
Product leadership strategy, 70–73
Promotion, 39, 54, 87. See also promotion
Relationship with target customer, 32–33, 36, 43–44
Retained customers, 50–54
Transactional vs. relational purchase, 61–66
Wants vs. needs, 47–48, 49, 50–51, 52, 54–55
3. When is the sale
About this step, 26–27, 28
Broad customer base and, 55
Buying process, 50–53, 85, 112. See also buying
Consumer to retained customer model, 51, 53–54
Customer urgency, 54–55
Marketing investment, 54
Needs vs. wants, 47–48, 49, 50–51, 52
Perception, 47–48
Quality–speed–price triangle, 62–65
Time and technology, 26–27
Timing is everything, 47–49, 54–55
Transactional vs. relational purchases, 61–66
Trigger to purchase, 113–114, 116
4. Where is the sale
About this step, 26–27, 28, 40
Customer determines place, 57–58
Global sales, 26–27
New vs. existing products, 39, 40
Online marketplace, 57–58, 59–60. See also online marketplace
Physical location, 57–58, 59–60. See also physical location
Promotion of where, 58–60, 85, 87
Transactional vs. relational purchases, 61–66
As transaction enabler, 25, 26

5. Why
About this step, 27–28, 69
Employees asking why, 69–70, 71–73, 78, 116
Importance of, 69–70
Landmines into lessons, 74
Leadership, 74–77
Price/value equation, 93, 114. See also price; value
Problem–solution of product, 38–39
Strategic style of business, 70–73
Trigger to purchase, 113–114
6. How promoted or packaged
About this step, 28
Attracting new customers, 102–103, 104–106, 110
Buying process, 85
Packaging, 25, 39, 40, 87
Price/value equation, 93
Promotion, 83. See also promotion
Promotional mix, 84, 86–87
Promotion communication, 87
Promotion goals, 85, 86–87
Trigger to purchase, 113–114
Unique selling proposition, 81–83
7. Price for profit. See also profit
Fair pricing, 93–94
Features your customers value, 37, 40–41
Lower cost or increase value, 92–93
Lowest bidder, 90
New vs. existing products, 39
Price/value equation, 93, 114
Problem-solution versus, 39
Profit must exist, 24–25, 26, 29, 91–92, 96
Promotional mix, 87
Purchasing decisions and, 51
Quality–speed–price triangle, 62–65
Strategies of pricing, 40
Supply and demand, 94–95, 96–97
"Sweet spot" of pricing, 24–25, 29
Transactional vs. relational purchase, 61–66
Variable pricing, 96–97
Adjustments for big impact, 112–117
Crime dramas using, 119. See also TV crime dramas
Insights gained, 20, 23
Landmines into lessons, 74
Model of framework, 22, 23
Overview, 5, 22, 28, 119
Perspective for reflection, 19, 22, 123, 132
Roadmap companion guidebook, 132
Franchise success, 21

G
Genius and talent, 30
Glenn, John
On learning from each other, 99
On lowest bidders, 90
Goethe, Johann Wolfgang von
On starting today, 4
Good as enemy of great, 101–102
Good to Great (Collins), 101
Goodyear, 48
Google's Ad Words, 60
Griffith, Andy (Matlock), 88
Grocery shopping variety, 27

Growth
Attracting new customers, 102–103, 104–106, 110
Customer identification, 34
Revenue greater than expenses, 25–26
Strategies for, 104–106
Top-line importance, 115–117
Gubman, Edward L.
The Talent Solution, 72, 73

H
Happy Days (TV show), 9
Homicide: Life on the Street (TV show), 6, 134
Hostess Brands promoting where, 58–59
How promoted or packaged
About this step, 28
Attracting new customers, 102–103, 104–106, 110
Buying process, 85
Packaging, 25, 39, 40, 87
Price/value equation, 93
Promotion, 83. See also promotion
Consistent communication, 87
Promotional mix, 84, 86–87
Promotion goals, 85, 86–87
Trigger to purchase, 113–114
Unique selling proposition, 81–83

I
Icebergs and tools for, 107–109
Information
Customer information, 18. See also customers
Gathering for decision making, 5–6, 17
Gathering with why, 69
Innovator or follower, 43–44
Internet. See online marketplace
Ismay, Joseph Bruce (White Star Line), 108

J
JAG (TV show), 6, 44–45, 134
Johnson, Don (Nash Bridges), 97
Jumping the shark, 9

K
K-Cups, 43–44
Kelley, Brian (Keurig), 43–44
Keurig Green Mountain, 43–44
Key questions
Promotion, 83
Target customer identification, 32
Keystone Revenue Solutions, Inc., 2, 131
Know: who, what, when, where for profitable price, 18, 120
Know your customers, 44–45, 105–106
Customer intimacy strategy, 70–73
Failure to understand, 18, 31, 33
Kodak Company and change, 41

L
Law, Vernon
Experience as hard teacher, 10
Learning tricks vs. trade, 15
Law & Order (TV show), 6, 35, 78, 134
Laws
Business without profits, 98

Cash gone → business gone, 11, 15, 24–25, 27, 91
Ohm's Law, 21
Principles versus, 20–21
Supply and demand, 94–95, 96–97
Leadership establishing why, 74–77
Top-line importance, 115–117
Levinson, Richard (Murder She Wrote), 66
Lincoln, Abraham
On predicting future by creating it, 45
Lingo avoidance, 82
Link, William (Murder She Wrote), 66
Listening to customers
Leadership in great businesses, 75
Product development, 40, 42, 43–44
Prospects vs. suspects, 111–112
Lowe, Harold (Titanic), 108

M
Marketing
About this framework step, 28
Advertising campaigns, 83, 85–86. See also advertising
Affinity of customer and product, 52–54
Benefits not features, 38–39, 81, 92, 93
Broad vs. narrow customer base, 32–33, 34
Trigger to purchase, 113, 116
When and broad base, 55
Cash for sales costs, 25–26, 27, 110
Half-wasted expense, 100, 110
Marketing budget, 86
Prospects vs. suspects, 110–112
Internet marketing, 60
Never-ending challenge, 54, 81
Niche marketing, 34
Problem product solves, 37, 81, 86
Promotional mix, 84, 86–87. See also promotion
Ps of marketing, 17, 37, 91
Target customer identification, 23–25, 28, 31–32, 45
Questions to ask, 32
Timing is everything, 47–49
Transactional vs. relational purchase, 61–66
Transaction enablers, 25
Unique selling proposition, 81–83
Matlock (TV show), 6, 88, 134
McAvoy, Roy "Tin Cup"
On defining moments, 118
Message. See communication
Mistakes and decision paralysis, 2
Model of framework, 22, 23
Monson, Thomas S.
On glories of creation, 3
Motivation to buy
Price and purchasing decision, 51
Promotion goal, 86–87
Question for source of, 32
Want vs. need, 49, 50, 52
Murder She Wrote (TV show), 6, 54, 66, 134
"My K-Cups," 43–44

N
NASCAR fan marketing, 48
Nash Bridges (TV show), 6, 97–98, 134
Nationwide Insurance, 2, 14, 101, 103, 131

NCIS (TV shows), 44–45
Needs of customers, 18, 20, 25, 26, 28, 103–104
Profit versus, 106
Wants vs. needs, 47–48, 49, 50–51, 52
Nestle PurinaCare leadership, 75–77
Netflix and change, 42
Niche marketing, 34
N.Y.P.D. Blue (TV show), 6, 134

O
Ohm's Law, 21
Online marketplace
Driving traffic to website, 57, 58, 59
Internet marketing, 60
Owningagreatbusiness.com, 132
Physical location plus, 57–58
Physical location versus, 60, 62, 63
PPC improvement, 60
SEO improvement, 60
Transactional vs. relational purchase, 61–66
Operational excellence strategy, 70–73
Opportunities
Decision making and, 15
Dynamic world creating, 40
Missed
Change shoulda happened, 41–42
Day-to-day details, 17
Decision making, 15
Opening doors in front of you, 67
Supply and demand, 94–95
Opportunity costs, 93–94
Organizing principles. See also framework for success
Customer information, 18. See also customers
Violation as fatal, 8, 88, 98, 119
Overcoming the odds
Business profitability percentages, 123
Business survival percentages, 11
Life savings investment, 1
TV crime dramas, 6–7
Owningagreatbusiness.com, 132

P
Packaging
New vs. existing products, 39, 40
Promotional mix, 87
As transaction enabler, 25, 40
Parsons, Jack
On leadership, 74–75
Pay-per-clicks (PPC), 60
Peak pricing model, 96–97
Perception
Customer's of value, 48, 70, 105–106, 114, 116
Fair pricing, 93–94
Price/value equation, 93, 114
Timing and, 47–48
Perry Mason (TV show), 88
Perspective for reflection, 19, 22, 123, 132
Physical location
Online also, 57–58
Online versus, 60, 62, 63
Promotion of where, 58–59
Where is critical, 57, 59

Transactional vs. relational purchase, 61–66
Physics laws vs. principles, 20–21
Place
Customer determines, 57–58
Global sales, 26–27
New vs. existing products, 39, 40
Online marketplace, 57–58, 59–60. See also online marketplace
Physical location, 57–58, 59–60. See also physical location
Promotion of where, 58–60, 85, 87
Transactional vs. relational purchases, 61–66
As transaction enabler, 25, 26
When, 26–27, 28. See also when is the sale
Where, 26–27, 28, 40. See also where is the sale
PPC (pay-per-clicks), 60
PPG Industries, Inc. (Pittsburgh Plate Glass), 2, 33, 103, 114, 131
Premium Nails, 50
Price. See also profit
Customer's perception, 48, 70, 105–106, 114, 116
Fair pricing, 93–94
Features your customers value, 37, 40–41
Lower cost or increase value, 92–93
Lowest bidder, 90
New vs. existing products, 39
Price/value equation, 93, 114. See also value
Problem–solution versus, 39
Profit must exist, 24–25, 26, 29, 91–92, 96
Promotional mix, 87
Purchasing decisions and, 51, 52
Quality–speed–price triangle, 62–65
Strategies of pricing, 40
Variable pricing, 96–97
Supply and demand, 94–95, 96–97
"Sweet spot" of pricing, 24–25, 29
Transactional vs. relational purchase, 61–66
Principles. See also framework for success
Customer information, 18. See also customers
Laws versus, 20–21
As truth concentrated, 5, 20, 102
"Uncertainly Principle," 21
Violation as fatal, 8, 88, 98, 119
Problem solving
Customer buying process, 52, 92–93
Customer's needs, 18, 20, 25, 26, 28, 103–104
Profit versus, 106
Delegating, 72, 74
Employees as problem solvers, 72, 73, 104, 107
God left unsolved, 3
Premium Nails, 50
Promotion of problem solved, 37, 81, 86
Timing is everything, 47–49
Transactional vs. relational purchase, 61–66
Uncontrollable factors, 109–110
What is the product, 37–39, 44–45
Product. See what is the product
Product complacency, 40–42, 97
Product leadership strategy, 70–73
Profit
Business definition, 12, 13, 32, 91
Consumer to retained customer model, 51, 53–54
Customer needs versus, 106

Percentage of small businesses, 123
Sales must produce, 24–25, 26, 29, 91–92, 96
Target vs. Walmart, 115–117
Promotion
About this framework step, 28
Attracting new customers, 102–103, 104–106, 110
Buying process, 85, 86
Definition, 83
Goals of, 85, 86–87
Marketing budget, 86. See also advertising; marketing
Never-ending challenge, 54, 81
New vs. existing products, 39
Promotional mix, 84, 86–87
Questions to ask, 83
Relevancy importance, 84, 86–87
Timing of, 55
As transaction enabler, 25
Trigger to purchase, 113–114
Unique selling proposition, 81–83
Where to purchase, 58–60, 85, 87
Without it: nothing, 80
Prospects vs. suspects, 110–112
Publicity definition, 83. See also promotion
PurinaCare leadership, 75–77

Q
Questions to ask
Promotion, 83
Target customer identification, 32
Quotations
Abraham Lincoln
Predict future by creating it, 45
Arthur Schopenhauer
Talent and genius, 30
Buzz Aldrin
Opportunities open doors, 67
Right place, right time, 56
Charles Darwin
Change and survival, 41
Jack Parsons
Leadership in great businesses, 74–75
Johann Wolfgang von Goethe
Start today, 4
John Glenn
Learning from each other, 99
Lowest bidders, 90
John Wanamaker
Advertising expense half-wasted, 100, 110
Peter Drucker
Knowing customer so well, 36
P.T. Barnum
Promotion or nothing, 80
Thorough understanding of business, 89
Roy "Tin Cup" McAvoy
Defining moments, 118
Roz Savage
Do it, surprise yourself, 121
Thomas S. Monson
Glories of creation, 3
Vernon Law
Experience as hard teacher, 10
Learning tricks vs. trade, 15
Warren Bennis
On environment to flourish, 79
On talent and belief, 68

William Bruce Cameron
Counting vs. things that count, 16
Yogi Berra
Timing over power, 46

R
Rackham, Neil
SPIN Selling, 51, 52
Reflection for perspective, 19, 22, 123, 132
Relationships
Connecting to start, 7–8
Customer intimacy strategy, 70–73
Customers and businesses, 31, 107
Customers leaving, 11–12
Transactional vs. relational purchases, 61–66
Retained customers
Affinity, 52–53
Consumer to retained customer model, 51, 53–54
Disney theme parks, 97
As great businesses backbone, 50–51
Loss of, 102, 104–106, 107
Maximization of, 105, 107
Revenue generation project, 52–54
Roadmap companion guidebook, 132
Rush orders for business cards, 63

S
Sales
Cash for sales costs, 25–26, 27, 110
Half-wasted expense, 100, 110
Marketing budget, 86
Prospects vs. suspects, 110–112
Consumer to retained customer model, 51, 53–54
Customer determines where, 57–58
Never-ending challenge, 54, 81
Unique selling proposition, 81–83
Up selling or cross selling, 105–106
Savage, Roz
On doing it, surprising yourself, 121
Scarcity and price, 94–95
Schopenhauer, Arthur
On talent and genius, 30
SEO (search engine optimization), 60
Service experience
Customer needs outside of scope, 103–104
Employee disconnect, 70, 87
Physical location vs. online, 60, 62, 63
Transactional vs. relational purchase, 61–66
7-P Framework. See framework for success
6 Ps of marketing, 91
Smith, Adam
The Wealth of Nations, 94
Southwest Airlines strategic style, 71–72
Speaking engagement topics, 131
SPIN Selling (Rackham), 51, 52
Stater Bros Markets, 103, 131
Staying power, 6
Step back for perspective, 19, 22, 123, 132
Storytelling
5W's + H, 5–6, 17, 119
Sharing with Lorin Young, 120
TV crime dramas, 6–7, 17, 119
Strategic style of business, 70–73
Success planning, 9
Supply and demand, 94–95, 96–97
Suspects vs. prospects, 110–112
"Sweet spot" of pricing, 24–25, 29

T
Talent and genius, 30
The Talent Solution (Gubman), 72, 73
Target customer identification, 23–25, 28, 31–35, 45
Exercise to avoid business failure, 124
As key, 23–24, 35, 36
Prospects vs. suspects, 110–112
Questions to ask, 32
Trigger to purchase, 113–114
Where purchases occur, 58, 59–60
Target vs. Walmart performance, 115–117
Television success stories. See TV crime dramas
Time and technology, 26–27
Timing is everything, 47–49. See also When is the sale
Blessing for Buzz Aldrin, 56
Titanic, icebergs, and tools, 107–109
Tools for the job, 108–109
Top-line importance, 115–117
"Touch." See service experience
Transactions
Enablers, 25–26
Transactional vs. relational purchase, 61–66
Treacy, Michael
Discipline of Market Leaders, 70
Truth. See principles
TV crime dramas
Connecting with customers, 7
"How" importance, 88
Leadership, 78
Promotional decisions, 54
Revenue vs. costs, 97–98
Storytelling, 6–7, 17, 119
Success of, 6–7
Success spawns success, 44–45
Success via framework, 119
5W's + H, 17
Target customer identification, 35
Violating principles, 9
"Where" importance, 66

U
"Uncertainly Principle," 21
Uncontrollable factors, 109–110
Unique selling proposition (USP), 81–83
Up-selling, 105–106

V
Value
Business as exchange of, 12, 13
Framework for success, 22, 23–27
Customer perception of, 48, 70, 105–106, 114, 116
Employees adding, 38, 60, 66, 70
Price perception, 93–94
Price/value equation, 93, 114
Quality–speed–price triangle, 62–66
Strategic style from, 70–73

Transactional vs. relational purchase, 61–66
Unique selling proposition, 81–83
Value pricing model, 96–97
Veterinary Pet Insurance (VPI), 1, 33, 52–54, 60, 75, 103, 131
Vistaprint and rush orders, 63
Visually compelling graphics, 39

W

Walker, Texas Ranger (TV show), 6, 134
Walmart vs. Target performance, 115–117
Walt Disney theme park pricing, 96–97
Wanamaker, John
On advertising expense half-wasted, 100, 110
Wants vs. needs, 47–48, 49, 50–51, 52
The Wealth of Nations (Smith), 94
What is the product
About this step, 25–26, 28
Benefits not features, 38–39
Broad or narrow customer base, 32–33, 34
Trigger to purchase, 113, 116
"When" and broad base, 55
Buying process, 50–53
Exercise to avoid business failure, 124
Follower vs. innovator, 43
Growth strategies, 105–106
New vs. existing, 38, 39–40
Packaging, 25, 39, 40, 87
Place, 40. See also place
Price, 40. See also price
Problem–solution, 37–39, 48–49
Product development, 40–42, 50, 97
Product leadership strategy, 70–73
Promotion, 39, 54, 87. See also promotion
Relationship with target customer, 32–33, 36, 43–44
Retained customers, 50–54
Transactional vs. relational purchase, 61–66
Wants vs. needs, 47–48, 49, 50–51, 52
When is purchase, 54–55
When is the sale
About this step, 26–27, 28
Broad customer base and, 55
Buying process, 50–53
Consumer to retained customer model, 51, 53–54
Customer urgency, 54–55
Marketing investment, 54
Needs vs. wants, 47–48, 49, 50–51, 52
Perception, 47–48
Quality–speed–price triangle, 62–65
Time and technology, 26–27
Timing is everything, 47–49, 54–55
Transactional vs. relational purchases, 61–66
Trigger to purchase, 113–114, 116
Where is the sale
About this step, 26–27, 28, 40
Customer determines, 57–58
Global sales, 26–27
New vs. existing products, 39, 40
Online marketplace, 57–58, 59–60. See also online marketplace
Physical location, 57–58, 59–60. See also physical location
Promotion of where, 58–60, 85, 87
Transactional vs. relational purchases, 61–66
As transaction enabler, 25, 26

Whitener Graphics and rush orders, 63
White Star Line and icebergs, 107–108, 109
Who is the customer. See also customers
About this step, 23–25, 28
Broad vs. narrow base, 32–33, 34
Trigger to purchase, 113, 116
When and broad base, 55
Target customer identification, 23–25, 28, 31–35, 45
Exercise to avoid business failure, 124
As key, 23–24, 35, 36
Prospects vs. suspects, 110–112
Questions to ask, 32
Trigger to purchase, 113–114
Where purchases occur, 58, 59–60
Why
About this step, 27–28, 69
Employees asking why, 69–70, 71–73, 78, 83, 87, 116
Importance of, 69–70
Landmines into lessons, 74
Leadership, 74–77
Price/value equation, 93, 114. See also price; value
Problem–solution of product, 38–39
Strategic style of business, 70–73
Trigger to purchase, 113–114
Wiersema, Fred
Discipline of Market Leaders, 70
Wolf, Dick (Law & Order), 35, 78
Workforce. See employees

X

The X-Files (TV show), 6, 134

Y

Young, Lorin, 131
Business builder, 1, 2, 131
Contact information, 120, 131
Design Dynamics
Broad customer base, 55
Customer care and loss, 109–110
Online marketing, 60
As owner, 1, 2, 13, 14, 103, 131
Supply and demand, 95
Target customer of, 34
Transactional vs. relational purchases, 61–66
Keystone Revenue Solutions, Inc., 2, 131
Nationwide Insurance, 2, 14, 101, 103, 131
Owningagreatbusiness.com, 132
PPG Industries, Inc., 2, 33, 103, 114, 131
Roadmap companion guidebook, 132
Speaking engagement topics, 131
Stater Bros Markets, 103, 131
Veterinary Pet Insurance, 1, 33, 52–54, 60, 75, 103, 131

www.ingramcontent.com/pod-product-compliance
Lightning Source LLC
Chambersburg PA
CBHW031419210526
45464CB00005B/1958